Rethinking Philosophy for Children

Radical Politics and Education
Series editors: Derek R. Ford and Tyson E. Lewis

With movements against oppression and exploitation heightening across the globe, radical activists and researchers are increasingly turning to educational theory to understand the pedagogical aspects of struggle. The Radical Politics and Education series opens a space at this critical juncture, one that pushes past standard expositions of critical education and critical pedagogy. Recognizing the need to push political and educational formulations into new theoretical and practical terrains, the series is an opportunity for activists, political thinkers, and educational philosophers to cross disciplinary divides and meet in common. This kind of dialogue is crucially needed as political struggles are increasingly concerned with questions of how to educate themselves and others, and as educational philosophy attempts to redefine itself beyond academic norms and disciplinary values. This series serves to facilitate new conversations at and beyond these borders.

Advisory Board:
Jodi Dean *(Hobart and William Smith Colleges, USA)*
Margret Grebowicz *(Goucher College, USA)*
Davide Panagia *(University of California, Los Angeles, USA)*
Patti Lather *(Ohio State University, USA)*
Nathan Snaza *(University of Richmond, USA)*
Stefano Harney *(Singapore Management University, Singapore)*

Also available in the series:
A History of Education for the Many: From Colonization and Slavery to the Decline of US Imperialism, Curry Malott
Against Sex Education: Pedagogy, Sex Work, and State Violence, Caitlin Howlett
Experiments in Decolonizing the University: Towards an Ecology of Study, Hans Schildermans

Forthcoming in the series:
A Voice for Maria Favela: An Adventure in Creative Literacy, Antonio Leal
Education, Society, and the Philosophy of Louis Althusser, David I. Backer
Queers Teach This!: Queer and Trans Pleasures, Politics, and Pedagogues, Adam J. Greteman

Rethinking Philosophy for Children

Agamben and Education as Pure Means

Tyson E. Lewis and Igor Jasinski

BLOOMSBURY ACADEMIC
LONDON • NEW YORK • OXFORD • NEW DELHI • SYDNEY

BLOOMSBURY ACADEMIC
Bloomsbury Publishing Plc
50 Bedford Square, London, WC1B 3DP, UK
1385 Broadway, New York, NY 10018, USA
29 Earlsfort Terrace, Dublin 2, Ireland

BLOOMSBURY, BLOOMSBURY ACADEMIC and the Diana logo are trademarks of
Bloomsbury Publishing Plc

First published in Great Britain 2022
This paperback edition published in 2023

Copyright © Tyson E. Lewis and Igor Jasinski, 2022

Tyson E. Lewis and Igor Jasinski have asserted their right under the Copyright,
Designs and Patents Act, 1988, to be identified as Author of this work.

Series design by Adriana Brioso
Cover image © bortonia/iStock

This work is published subject to a Creative Commons Attribution Non-commercial No Derivatives Licence. You may share this work for non-commercial purposes only, provided you give attribution to the copyright holder and the publisher.

Bloomsbury Publishing Plc does not have any control over, or responsibility for, any thirdparty websites referred to or in this book. All internet addresses given in this book were correct at the time of going to press. The author and publisher regret any inconvenience caused if addresses have changed or sites have ceased to exist, but can accept no responsibility for any such changes.

A catalogue record for this book is available from the British Library.

Library of Congress Cataloging-in-Publication Data

Names: Lewis, Tyson E., author. | Jasinski, Igor, author.
Title: Rethinking philosophy for children: Agamben and education as pure
means / Tyson E. Lewis and Igor Jasinski.
Description: London; New York: Bloomsbury Academic, 2021. |
Series: Radical politics and education |
Includes bibliographical references and index. |
Identifiers: LCCN 2021007680 (print) | LCCN 2021007681 (ebook) |
ISBN 9781350133570 (hardback) | ISBN 9781350133587 (ebook) |
ISBN 9781350133594 (epub)
Subjects: LCSH: Children–Language. | Agamben, Giorgio, 1942-
Classification: LCC LB1139.L3 L473 2021 (print) |
LCC LB1139.L3 (ebook) | DDC 372.6–dc23
LC record available at https://lccn.loc.gov/2021007680
LC ebook record available at https://lccn.loc.gov/2021007681

ISBN: HB: 978-1-3501-3357-0
PB: 978-1-3502-1682-2
ePDF: 978-1-3501-3358-7
eBook: 978-1-3501-3359-4

Series: Radical Politics and Education

Typeset by Integra Software Services Pvt. Ltd.

To find out more about our authors and books visit www.bloomsbury.com
and sign up for our newsletters.

Contents

Preface	vi
Acknowledgements	ix
Introduction: Philosophy for Infancy	1
1 Demand	21
2 Rules	45
3 Adventure	61
4 Love	77
5 Happiness	97
6 Anarchy	117
Notes	137
References	149
Index	155

Preface

Why write a book that attempts to return to the origins of the practice known as Philosophy for/with Children (P4C) using a philosopher, Giorgio Agamben, whose ideas many consider inaccessible, impractical, and obscure? Why write a book that P4C practitioners and other educators are likely to find too abstract and not helpful (irrelevant?) to their practice, that academic philosophers will dismiss as being a form of applied philosophy (and, thus, not to be taken seriously), and that philosophers of education will regard as too theoretical and not enough focused on educational practice or policy (or at least not on a practice that matters in mainstream education)? In short, why write a book that is likely to displease almost all audiences that might want to read such a book in the first place?

Our answer is simple: love. We fell in love with the experience of a certain way of doing philosophy with children, loving this experience for whatever it is (letting it be whatever it is), feeling a passion to articulate our experience and why it is something that we want others—students and educators alike—to experience as well and why it is worth doing so in an educational setting (such as a school). What the practice consists of and the reasons we fell in love with it are, simply stated, that it allows students to come in contact with their potentiality for speaking and the demand this potentiality places upon them. Although this was self-evident to us, we did not find adequate resources in the existing P4C literature to articulate what was so *singular* and *special* about our experience. We found a lot of discussion about evaluating students' speech for signs of reasonableness, discussions of developing certain dispositions toward citizenship and democracy, and a pragmatic appreciation for the power of critical thinking. As desirable as these ends appear to be, it was P4C's unique ability to suspend ends (reasonableness, democracy) in order to turn attention to means that captured our imagination. It was the means as such that we began to fall in love with, the ability to speak and think full stop. And it was for this reason that an articulation with Agamben seemed necessary, as Agamben's philosophical interests rest on understanding means *without* ends.

Let's consider a conversation of a group of sixth graders, discussing the question: "What is time?"

"Without time there would still be time but we couldn't measure anything."

"Without time we would all be frozen. Time is not a real thing. It's not mental. Bugs are not frozen in time. They move, they have a life, and they can sense time."

"Bugs have a sense of time because they have a sleep-wake cycle. Maybe time can go in reverse?"

"Without time we would still be living. We wouldn't be frozen. We would be moving but we would have no motivation or purpose. You could show up to school once a month."

"We would still be moving, but things would just be more disorganized. We would still have a sense of time because we know when its light/dark, night/day."

"Someone said that people survived before there was time, but there is never 'before time.' There is a time before we started counting time, but there was still time."

"We are not talking about time itself. To find out what time is, we have to find out how it would be without it. Also: before time was created the universe wasn't created."

"Before we were created there was time, but it had no meaning."

"Time is just the way we look at things."

"Without time everything would go out of whack and fall into chaos."

We may wonder: Where is this going? What are the students learning? What are the ends to which they are directed (or should be directed)? As teachers, we might question at what point we need to intervene to make sure that they get better at this kind of dialogue, become more logical or reasonable, and learn to make better arguments. As researchers, we might ask what kind of data this dialogue provides and how it might be coded to uncover the efficacy of this particular pedagogical approach to critical thinking and argumentation? Yet our point is more basic: there is something about letting students speak, about abandoning them to their capacities for speech, about enabling them to adventure with saying what can be thought and think what can be said. And there is nothing we—as teachers or facilitators—could say that would add to their experience and might, in fact, diminish or even destroy it. In this sense, we merely want to share this moment of sharing with you, without analysis or interpretation, without turning speech into data or evidence (of growth, development, or progress in a certain direction). We want to share the excitement of the moment, not evaluate it.

At stake here is preserving a space and time in education for *infancy*—for the experience of language as a means (speakability, communicability) and how this, in the end, proves to be *the* foundational philosophical experience. As paradoxical as it might sound, to make sure philosophy for children remains philosophical, we have to safeguard it as an *impractical* practice for preserving means over and above all ends. We have to embrace its most infantile manifestations. And this is what the literature in the field of P4C seems to continually miss—always orienting infancy *toward* something deemed relevant, necessary, or preferable (according to a certain standard of reasonableness or democratic participation).

We wrote this book to articulate how the kind of experience made possible by an unguided form of philosophical inquiry (letting students speak) is (has been for us)—first and foremost—a source of happiness. As such, it allowed us to glimpse the potential of education not as just a means toward the realization of a happy life, but as the place and time wherein happiness can and does suddenly make a guest appearance, transforming learning into a moment of studious play. While the following text might seem like a critique P4C, it is not. Rather, it is a return to origins in order to redeem what is most exciting, joyous, and adventurous when adults and children attend to the unique demand placed upon them by their shared infancy.

Acknowledgements

The authors would like to acknowledge all of our students who have experimented with various iterations of P4C and P4I with us over the years. We would also like to acknowledge our editor, Dr. Anne Keefe, for providing critical feedback on both the form and content of the book.

Introduction: Philosophy for Infancy

Today we live in a "learning society."[1] Within a flexible, knowledge-driven, neoliberal economy, laborers must become "life-long learners" constantly optimizing their labor through reskilling, and likewise, learners have to orient themselves toward twenty-first-century skills needed by the neoliberal economy. Thus, the dominance of discourses and practices of learning dovetails with certain economic needs to the point where learning and laboring become largely indistinct (or at least mutually reinforcing). Likewise, Gert Biesta argues that the learning prevalent today transforms educational relations into economic transactions in which "the teacher, the educator, or the educational institution is seen as the provider, that is, the one who is there to meet the needs of the learner, and where education itself becomes a commodity—a 'thing'—to be provided or delivered by the teacher or educational institution and to be consumed by the learner."[2] On both accounts, learning is not simply naturally given but is a historically specific manifestation of education according to certain economic logics. Whether one is referring to authentic learning, deep learning, situated learning, or standardized learning, there is a consistent economy of forces at play: (a) there is an intention to learn that (b) informs the selection and planning of experiences through which (c) growth, development, or progress is measured. This learning process is verified by assessment, both formal and informal.[3] The economy of learning means that learning is a form of educational life that can be *managed* and, by extension, made increasingly operative. Just as capitalism has an uncanny ability to absorb back into itself all forms of resistance, so too do learning discourses and practices have a similar power to take all notions of education that fall outside its economy and appropriate them, instrumentalize them, and orient them toward measurable outcomes. While there is nothing about learning that is, in itself, harmful, when learning becomes a hegemonic force wedded to neoliberal economic logics it becomes increasingly dangerous, absorbing alternatives into itself, and thus erasing forms of educational life that do not abide by measurement.

One such practice that is now increasingly under threat is Philosophy for Children (P4C). While proponents of this practice might argue that P4C is under threat from the *outside*, we would argue that it is also under threat from the *inside*, meaning that to adapt to the learning society, it too has become part of a larger learning apparatus. Developed by Matthew Lipman in the 1970s, the founding assumption of P4C was to introduce philosophy into schools as a practice that lets children *do* philosophy through group dialogue, allowing them to become active thinkers by developing critical and reasoning skills that become the foundation for democratic development and civic engagement.[4] According to Lipman, Ann Margaret Sharp, and Frederick S. Oscanyan, the P4C facilitator aids in the development of such skills and dispositions by promoting a certain kind of talking—philosophical dialogue—that consists of eliciting opinions, asking for clarifications, calling for interpretation, seeking consistency when needed, requiring definitions, pinpointing assumptions, indicating fallacies, asking students to say how they know, examining alternatives, grouping ideas, and suggesting possible alternatives. Through collective philosophical dialogue concerning issues such as right and wrong, truth and falsehood, rules and standards, beauty and ugliness, and so forth, children develop logical and ethical thinking as the internalization of dialogic procedures. The facilitator should not spoon-feed children answers but help them ask and explore their own questions while steering them toward skill development and a desire to engage in further democratic dialogue: "Students are expected to be thoughtful and reflective, and increasingly reasonable and judicious."[5] Overall, there is an emphasis on the goal (reasonableness), on something that is being sought (*quaerere* = to ask, gain, seek, related to "quest"), on moving forward, on advancing (the conversation), on looking for something through reasonable reflection. "[T]he community of inquiry," Lipman writes, "is not aimless. It is a process that aims at producing a *product*—at some kind of settlement or judgment, however partial and tentative this may be."[6] Although Lipman and Sharp emphasize a holistic notion of a "well-tempered life,"[7] Sharp makes it clear that the "ultimate criterion" that guides action—and the actions within the community of inquiry, in particular—ought to be "reasonableness."[8] Sharp then draws on Pierce to articulate the following formulation of the work of P4C in relation to self-transformation through reasonableness: "[T]he self is an evolving construction that is (a) oriented towards the future, (b) a developmental teleology, a pursuit of purposes or plans in which genuinely novel directions can and do emerge. And (c) during any moment of life, the self is first and foremost understood in the process of self-correction in which some species of meaning is evolving."[9] Notions of reasonableness and the well-tempered life have been expanded over the years to include critical, creative, and caring thinking,[10] but the key point here is that the content of what it means to live such a life is determined *in advance* of any given P4C session. The ensuing dialogue is therefore organized around a particular goal or end toward which progress, development, or growth can be assessed. In this sense, P4C is an opportunity to *learn* about the well-tempered life through a particular experience of reasonable speech in the presence of others.

There have been a number of critiques addressing the instrumental nature of this more or less "traditional" view of P4C and its connections to the logic of the learning society.[11] Biesta, for example, writes that philosophy in P4C is "deployed as an instrument that is supposed to work upon individuals so that they can develop and/or acquire certain qualities, capacities and skills."[12] As an alternative, Biesta proposes to use "exposure" as a central educational concept. "Exposure," he writes, "is … not about the revelation of a unique, pre-existing identity; … Exposure does not produce; exposure interrupts, … bringing about an experience of not knowing."[13] Drawing on Foucault's theory of truth telling, Nancy Vansieleghem advocates a reconceptualization of the P4C facilitator as a parrhesiast who "does not understand speaking, thinking or seeing as skills one has to acquire—say, through 'learning by doing'—but as a work upon the self … in this sense the parrhesiast does not coordinate a discursive scene or focus an argument"[14] but rather puts the self at risk. The facilitator thus cannot take an external or meta-position with reference to laws of logic or reasonableness outside of the present educational situation. And Thomas Storme and Joris Vlieghe observe: "Of course it seems convenient, if not practically inevitable, to define philosophy (for/with) children as a set of practices, competences, methods, and skills that have a specific content and deliver specific goals." Yet, this also renders it "subservient to the existing regime, i.e. as [merely] an interesting addition to the set of competences provided by the existing curriculum."[15] At stake in such critiques is a desire to separate P4C from the logic of learning, which is oriented toward the production and evaluation of learning outputs/products in the name of progress, growth, or development toward predefined goals or ends that exist outside the community of inquiry.

On the other hand, some argue that the only way to make a place for P4C in today's strict, standardized classroom is to empirically quantify its efficacy in promoting reasoning/argumentation skills.[16] From this vantage point, philosophy must be made *more instrumental* and *more functional* in order to survive as a practice within the learning society. Through measurement, the efficacy of P4C dialogue can be objectively evaluated in terms of learning outputs. Yet we argue that this interpretation of P4C is precisely what must be avoided in order to safeguard what is truly *experimental and philosophical* in P4C dialogue. Focusing primarily on the improvement of argumentation and reasoning skills as the main benefit (the active ingredients) of P4C, it is only consistent that Alena Reznitskaya et al. would *de-emphasize* the philosophical dimension in P4C by referring to P4C as "an educational environment called philosophy for children."[17] To simply transform P4C into another educational environment is to prematurely abandon what we see as the radical core of the practice itself and capitulate to the necessities for measurable and maximally operable outcomes that fuel the economy of the learning society.

What we want to offer in this book is a reevaluation of the potentiality of P4C. Instead of simply negating the traditional view of P4C (as critics and/or proponents of the learnification of P4C are apt to do), what we want to do is return to certain primary texts (predominantly those written by Lipman and Sharp) in order to redeem what remains latent within them, on the margins, and in the fringes. In this sense, we are adopting the philosophical methodology of Giorgio Agamben who argues that the role of philosophy is always to return to the untapped potentiality of a concept, action, event, or theory. To redeem such potentiality means that standard/normative understandings and applications should be temporarily rendered inoperative so that new, unforeseen alternative ideas and uses can come to the foreground. In this case, what we propose, à la Agamben, is a messianic reading of P4C where the messianic is not an overturning of the old for the new but rather the "world itself, with a slight adjustment, a meager difference."[18] This meager difference will, we argue, make all the difference in defining what is at stake when children speak. Rather than see what becomes of P4C "post-Lipman"[19] we want to stay with Lipman for a moment longer. The result will not produce something new—some radically new and drastically different alternative or set of helpful tips or updated curricular suggestions. Instead, the meager difference sought after will provide the reader with insight into certain marginal possibilities for thinking about what is philosophical in P4C that is threatened by the rise in learning discourses and practices (both from without and from within). The resulting portrait of P4C will be both familiar and strange, different and the same, or just different enough to continue to use the "philosophical" means in P4C.

The turn to Agamben as an ally in this adventure is not unprecedented within the P4C literature. There is passing reference to Agamben in the work of Walter Omar Kohan, for instance.[20] But what we want to offer here is a more systematic approach that not only references certain ideas cribbed from

Agamben's work, but also attempts to deploy his method of doing philosophy. While it is difficult to summarize Agamben's method, there are largely three interconnected dimensions of his method that we will use in order to think P4C differently. First, there is the structural dimension. Agamben likes to think of philosophy in magnetic terms. On every magnet, there are positive and negative poles and in between there is a zone of indistinction, inoperativity, suspension, or neutralization. This is the neutral point on a magnet that is neither positive nor negative yet somehow contains within itself both pairs of opposites simultaneously. For Agamben, this is the point of potentiality. Our question will always be to find this neutralization point in the discourses and practices surrounding P4C in order to return the theory and practice back to its philosophical origin (which has been put in jeopardy by accommodating the learning society). There is also a temporal or messianic dimension to his method. Agamben will frequently make the claim that we, as a civilization, have lost something (our gestures, our ability to celebrate, our relationship to the world, or, most importantly, our relationship with language as meaningful). But we cannot simply return to the past. Instead, Agamben argues that we have to redeem that in the past that *never was*—the latent potentiality in the past. It is our intuition that a close read of Lipman and Sharp—as representatives of the first wave of P4C theorists and practitioners—will enable us to discover this latent potentiality and to reclaim it for the present. As suggested above, this will not necessitate drastic, revolutionary moves, but rather slight adjustments that nevertheless will change everything. And finally, there is an educational dimension to Agamben's work that is worth pointing out. He often pinpoints a structure of capture that separates, divides, or negates something and then attempts to render inoperative this mechanism of capture. Rendering inoperative a mechanism of capture returns us to that which we were separated from, and in doing so, opens what remains up for contemplation or study. This gesture of study has been an entry point for articulating Agamben with education,[21] and, in this book, we will argue that it enables us to find points of connection and separation with PC4.

P4C is worth redeeming precisely because it sees children as capable of philosophical dialogue and even philosophical creativity.[22] On the one hand, this is a radical gesture that interrupts a consistent bias in education: that young children cannot be philosophers, cannot think reasonably.[23] Emphasis on speech as a tool for developing reasonableness prematurely forecloses on a more basic and fundamental experiment, or what Agamben refers to as an "*experimentum linguae*"[24]—an experiment that concerns the very existence of speech itself. P4C accepts the existence of speech as the taken-for-granted background out of which a community of inquiry can come to define itself, its goals, and its procedures. Yet for Agamben, the real philosophical experience is first and foremost the surprise at the appearance of speech as such, full stop. As Agamben states, "The only content of the *experimentum* is that *there is language*."[25] This might seem rather obvious, but for Agamben, it is a radical achievement for two reasons.

First, Agamben pinpoints a central problem in Western metaphysics: an emphasis on binary negation. Examples of a critical engagement with binary logic are found throughout Agamben's work. For instance, in linguistics, we have the separation between *phone* (animal voice) and *logos* (human language); in discourse we have a separation between philosophy (which does not possess its object but knows it) and poetry (which possess its object without knowing it); in politics we have a separation between bare life (*zoe*) and the life of the citizen (*bios*); and in biology we have the separation between the human and the animal. In each case, identity of one side of a binary pair is predicated on the negation of the other side. The danger here is that negation involves *sacrifice*. For instance, to be constituted as human, signs of the nonhuman animal must be negated and externalized (even if this is an impossible gesture). Agamben's experiment in language attempts to find a starting point for thought that is purely *affirmative* rather than *negative*. This is an experiment in impossible syntheses or points of indistinction that trouble any attempt to determine and fix binary oppositions. Returning to the image of the magnet, to experiment, for Agamben, is to *neutralize* in order to repotentialize.

Second, for language to function as a tool of communication, it must presuppose a foundation that it *can never speak*. Language cannot seem to speak itself or speak its own speakability. Thus, what is actually outside of language is nothing other than its own potentiality to be spoken! An experiment in language, for Agamben, would thus have to be an experiment that does not negate such potentiality but rather figures out a way for this potentiality to pass into the act of speech without erasing itself.

Infancy is an experiment in language that attempts to overcome the impasse of Western metaphysics by returning language to its origins. Infancy is not the experience of speaking *some content* so much as the experience of the *ability to speak*. Infancy thus concerns the experience of the very limit of language—its speakability—without presupposing that this speakability is something beyond language (or inaccessible to language). To experiment with language means that the content of speech is precisely the potentiality of speech to be spoken. Whereas such potentiality is often assumed in order to be *consumed* in the act of speech as a sacrifice, what Agamben is after is a form of speech that is infantile insofar as it embodies or exemplifies its own possibility by continually deactivating or rendering inoperative the binary that attempts to institute a separation over and against potentiality.

Here we must define potentiality. To be in potential means that something can and cannot come into being, that it is equal parts impotentiality and potentiality. Drawing on but also moving beyond Aristotle's original description of potentiality, Agamben writes, "Beings that exist in the mode of potentiality *are capable of their own impotentiality*" in such a way that "sensation is in relation to anesthesia, knowledge to ignorance, vision to darkness."[26] Instead of attempting to exhaust potentiality by having it pass without remainder into an actualization, Agamben is attempting to think a mode of being that is *in potential* without sacrificing impotentiality. Thus, Agamben's question is, how can one preserve impotentiality without it being negated by an act? Paradoxically, Agamben summarizes this as follows: "What is truly potential is thus what has exhausted all its impotentiality in bringing it wholly into the act as such."[27] Whereas traditional philosophy presupposes impotentiality as that dimension of potentiality that must be sacrificed in the name of the act, Agamben searches for phenomena that do not exhaust potentiality but rather allow *impotentiality* to pass wholly into an actualization. Paradoxically, this means Agamben is interested in acts that deactualized themselves or deactualized actualizations. Such an act would not be based on negation (of impotentiality) nor would it be an act oriented toward completing or fulfilling a telos.

Examples of impotentiality passing into an act are varied throughout Agamben's work and include the following. First, certain artists express their impotentiality in an act insofar as they are incapable of not performing/making/doing. When a musician plays an instrument with passion, he/she cannot *not* play. Thus, the musician gives him- or herself over to the playing, letting impotentiality (the ability to not not-play) pass into the act without negating it. Second, "preferring not to" do *x*, *y*, or *z* expresses impotentiality through a deactivated or neutralized gesture that does not reach its goal or fulfill its purported destiny. Think here of Bartleby the Scrivener who "would prefer not to" complete his job as a copyist, but in so doing he does not pass beyond the occupation of copyist, instead he becomes a copyist *as not* a copyist. In other words, he is not a copyist who fulfills the function of a copyist in terms of outputs or quotas and yet prefers not to abandon or negate his position in the firm as a copyist. Thus, he is an employee that is no longer defined in terms of work done or what is accomplished. There is a hollowing out of the content of being a copyist to the point where the role serves no function within an economy yet remains somehow in use through Bartleby's enigmatic gestures. Third, studying, for Agamben, offers a moment of stupification in which the studier experiences his/her capability to think confronting itself. Study is the contemplation of potentiality (in general) and infancy (in particular). This is a thought whose content is its own possibility or whose possibility passes into the form of content without separation or sacrifice of that which remains impotential within thought. All of these forms critically undermine binaries between activity and passivity (cannot not do/be/make), potentiality and actuality (preferring not), capability and incapability (contemplation), and in the process suggest a form-of-life that does not negate impotentiality but rather allows impotentiality to express itself through various forms of suspension and inoperativity.

For us, philosophy with and for children offers another experience of such impotentiality: infancy. Infancy is an experience of one's potentiality to speak passing into speech without negation and without destiny. Instead of negating its origin in order to communicate this or that message or skill or developmental telos, speech only communicates its own capacity for communication. The medium—speech—is the message, as Marshall McLuhan might have said. This means that speech is not oriented toward a specific end—as in the teleologically certified cultivation of reasonableness or care or democratic values. Rather it is oriented toward itself, its own condition of possibility, its own facticity, its auto-affection. Infant speech has no destiny (a direction it is supposed to develop toward) and no negation (a sacrifice of its origins). Instead, it is a kind of speech that brings into speech that which cannot be spoken (the inability to be able to and not to speak).

To theorize the potential for P4C to be an experiment in and of infancy, we will draw heavily on Agamben's work. Our argument is that the redemption of P4C necessitates a shift from a community of inquiry (as the dialogic model underlying P4C) to a *community of infancy* (P4I). It is a community because it is a common experience of language. And it is a community of infancy because this common experience of language emphasizes language's speakability, its potentiality. In theorizing the practices of community of infancy, what will emerge is an experiment in language that is shared. P4C has a long-established record of advocating for a conceptualization of children as capable of philosophical dialogue in the name of democratic citizenship and care ethics. Our book takes up the practice of P4C and reconstitutes it according to the philosophy of Agamben in order to create a new practice: P4I. The key difference between P4C and P4I is a noninstrumental approach to education that does not focus on learning how to be reasonable (through critical, creative, and caring thinking) as a specific destiny of speech so much as the more basic and fundamental experience of a child's incapacity to speak (the experience of infancy) as the primary philosophical and poetic experiment. This means that P4C can no longer be thought of in terms of destiny (producing reasonable citizens, for instance) or negation (the overcoming of *phone* and its replacement by *logos* or immaturity by maturity or irrational by rational speech). Instead, education emerges as a means without a prescribed destiny or as a pure means wherein children are exposed in a new way to the capacities they already have in the present moment: the potentiality for speaking. The upshot of this practice is that education can no longer be thought of as preparation for a life to come (democratic citizenship, for instance) so much as exposure to that which is closest and most familiar yet at the same time and for these very same reasons farthest away and most difficult to grasp. Without an end in sight to orient the practice, the educational logic of learning underlying and supporting P4C is rendered inoperative. What is left is an education of pure means, or an education in and of potentiality.

Even if we find kinship with critics of P4C, we would also like to emphasize that our project is not a rejection or even negation of the original practice. In fact, we find much in the traditional approach worth returning to and reevaluating through a messianic lens. For instance, Lipman's earliest conceptualizations of P4C emphasize the centrality of metacognition. He encourages students to think about thinking or to learn how they learn. He concludes that teachers must help even very young children foster metacognition for "children are unlikely to reason better if they cannot reason about how they reason."[28] In this sense, community of inquiry is a process in thinking about the preconditions for thinking (inferencing about how one inferences, for instance). We agree with Lipman's general point here. Bearing in mind Agamben's notions of potentiality and infancy, we can argue that P4I is not an abandonment of Lipman's articulation of P4C so much as its development, focusing explicitly on the need to offer children experiences of the *potentiality* for speaking. Infancy is an inquiry into the potentiality for speaking or speaking's speakability. It does not concern what is said or how it ought to be said but rather *that* something can be said (speakability). It is therefore metacognitive. Or, as Agamben puts it, "philosophy is concerned with the pure existence of language, independent of its real properties [grammar]."[29] An experience of language's speakability (its pure existence) should be valued. This is not about learning a metalanguage higher than the language of everyday speech (as in Lipman's model of critical self-reflection) but rather an exposure to the word's speakability, its mediality. This is an immanent rather than transcendent model of metacognition. Instead of a mere means to an end (the development of reason or citizenship skills) through a particular metacognitive grammar and/or set of logical processes, speakability is a pure means, exposing the child to the contingencies of being a speaking being or the contingencies of language that do not have a destiny. Infancy resists the temptation to transform P4C into an instrument of the learning society. And it does so by being metacognitive but without an end.

Metacognition enables philosophy to have a broad perspective on the disciplines. For instance, Lipman argues that philosophy concerns "learning to think about the thinking in the disciplines"[30] while at the same time transcending any discipline-specific content. In this way, philosophy remains generic. There is, in this sense, something about philosophy that is not reducible to domain-specific forms of inquiry. Of course, Lipman recognizes the utility of philosophy in the disciplines as a critical tool for analyzing the founding assumptions of specific discourses, yet he also wants to retain a sense of philosophy's transdisciplinary status, and thus, its unique ability to explore the essence of inquiry as such. For this very reason, philosophy can be an inquiry into inquiry itself, a thinking about the preconditions of thought (metacognition). Likewise, Agamben is interested in turning to philosophers and thinkers who somehow move beyond their disciplines toward a new science or experiment with language that individual disciplines might prevent them from accomplishing. A good example of this is Aby Warburg whose practice Agamben describes as a "nameless science" that can only be understood "as a unified effort, across and beyond art history, directed toward a broader science for which he could not find a definite name."[31] The nameless science will have to remain so until it can "overcome the fatal divisions and false hierarchies separating not only the human sciences from one another but also artworks from the *studia humaniora* and literary creation from science."[32] In this sense, Agamben is similar to but much more radical than Lipman in his quest for a science or experiment that somehow lives within the paradoxical zone between science and literature, criticism and creation, prose and poetry. Only from this vantage point can an experiment with language discover that which all the separate disciplines presuppose but, also, in the end, sacrifice: infancy or the potentiality within speech to be spoken.

Likewise, Lipman is keen on preserving what is philosophical in the experience of the community of inquiry. He warns against the mere reduction of philosophy to "thinking skills" that, for him, are "pseudo-philosophical."[33] We agree with Lipman, who, in many ways, anticipates the emergent critics of P4C outlined above. To hold onto the philosophical against the pseudo-philosophical or the nonphilosophical is to emphasize the wonder of philosophy. But wonder at what? For us, wonderment is first and foremost wonderment over the very ability to speak. *This* wonderment is what must be preserved. When Lipman and his coauthors over emphasize the teaching of reasoning, they *lend* themselves to instrumentalization (even while they argue against it). P4C can all too easily be appropriated by the learning society as a convenient tool for instructing children in argumentative skills. And this is not an accident as there are features within P4C that are amenable to such appropriation. Yet infancy cannot be instrumentalized. It is a pure potentiality to speak that is undestined and radically contingent. Thus, we have to pare down the practice of PC4 to its essential features in order to maintain the philosophical kernel at its heart and to open it up for new use beyond the learning society.

Use for Agamben is not reducible to functionality. Instead, use appears when an activity is freed up from instrumentality and a necessary relationship to an end. Drawing on the ancient writings of Lucretius, Agamben writes,

> [U]se seems to be completely emancipated from every relation to a predetermined end, in order to affirm itself as the simple relation to the living thing with its own body, beyond every teleology ... no organ was created in view of an end, neither the eyes for vision, nor the ears for hearing, nor the tongue for speech ... use precedes and creates their function.[34]

Use is found when (a) an old function or factical set of conditions is deactivated/rendered inoperative and (b) a potentiality is opened up (the ability to be and not to be according to a set function). Perhaps we can say that infantile speech is truly *useful speech* but only in so far as it has lost its function (and as such, its place within the economy of the learning society). Our worry is that under the hegemonic dominance of the learning society, P4C has become *too functional* (meaning that the ends are already set, the pedagogy already fixed, and the evaluation tools ready to be deployed to measure growth, development, or maturity toward reasonableness and democratic citizenship). But with increased functionality, P4C must sacrifice its own infancy. While skills might be maximized, the philosophical in P4C is minimized.

Interestingly, Lipman makes the observation that children's thinking "may not be quite so instrumental and operational in character"[35] as scientifically advanced or discipline-specific thinking. As such, they are full of wonder in ways that connect them to philosophy and its meta-questions. This, for Lipman, is precisely why children are amenable to the community of inquiry model. At the same time, the emphasis on becoming reasonable or cultivating values in traditional P4C tends to reduce this noninstrumental and inoperative nature of children's thinking to something that ought to be managed under the auspices of philosophy. For Agamben, on the other hand, it is precisely the noninstrumental and inoperative dimensions of children's thinking (and speaking) that actualize impotentiality in the form of infantile speech. On this reading, children's speech is not simply the starting point for development, growth, or progress toward reasonableness. Rather, it is a way of throwing into relief the origin of speaking's speakability that is present in all forms of speech yet denied. This is not something learned (under the guidance of a P4C facilitator) so much as something participants are exposed to through infantile babbling.

Lipman focuses on the problem of transmission as the defining problem facing education. Whereas the "standard" model of education focuses on "the transmission of knowledge from those who know to those who don't know," in the reflective model underlying P4C "the focus of the educational process is not on the acquisition of information but on the grasp of relationships within and among the subject matters under investigation."[36] In other words, there is a shift on transmitting modes of inquiry that can critically analyze subject matter and how they relate rather than on transmitting specific content. We would agree with Lipman's diagnosis. Indeed, transmission is at stake in schools—transmission between generations. Yet Lipman fails to see that focus on inquiry itself and its specific skills, dispositions, and so forth merely replaces one content (subject content) for another (procedural content). Faith in procedural content remains in the P4C model espoused by Lipman and tethers P4C to specific learning outcomes (this time in relation to increasing manifestations of reasonableness and judiciousness). We offer an alternative: instead of remaining focused on the transmission of content, we will turn to infancy as the *transmission of transmissibility*. In other words, the experience of infancy is the experience of transmissibility without content, the potentiality for transmission to happen as such through linguistic dialogue with others in a community.

Finally, Lipman emphasizes *dialogue* (and thus language) as central to the philosophical experience offered by the community of inquiry. We appreciate the insight offered by Sharp and Megan Jane Laverty that Lipman's traditional formulation can be criticized for often reducing reasonableness to the domain of logical argumentation (thus sacrificing other forms of discourse including stories, anecdotes, and so forth).[37] This line of criticism can be further extended to an overreliance on verbal forms of expression over other more embodied modes of discourse.[38] We also appreciate the focus on the role of the body in the community and its ethical implications. Yet at the same time, we feel that an emphasis on embodiment takes away from what is most unique in P4C: an experiment with language that happens through speaking and through linguistic mannerisms. Here Lipman's narrow focus on dialogic exchange ought to be retained as a defining feature of the practice. Whereas any number of progressive pedagogies include the body—and we are not denying that inquiry with children should do so as well—P4C is distinct in its focus on speech. Indeed, the most appropriate way to take into account the body is an emphasis on infancy in speech as that which resists the dichotomy between *phone* and *logos.* Ironically enough, when Sharp and Laverty *add* the body to the community of inquiry above and beyond dialogue, they subtly reproduce the split between body and language that lead to the sacrifice of the body in the first place. Likewise, Sharp and Laverty's insistence on a pedagogy of alterity/otherness should be anchored in speech, as the otherness that is discovered through speaking is not outside of speech but is the unspeakable kernel of speech within speech (its potentiality). As such, we want to maintain Sharp and Laverty's criticism of the instrumentalization/learnification of speech in the name of logical argumentation while also maintaining Lipman's focus on the linguistic aspects of P4C. In short, infancy as speech's (in)ability to speak itself ought to be preserved as the core of the practice.

In sum, Lipman hopes that P4C can *accomplish the work of learning* to be a reasonable, democratic citizen who is creative, caring, and critical. P4I on the other hand renders inoperative the work of learning and therefore restores to education its possibility, opening it up for new use. The practitioner of P4I no longer defines him- or herself in terms of a praxis or a work but by a potentiality and an inoperativity. And in so doing, a new form of educational life emerges that is predicated not on hope for a better tomorrow so much as happiness with the form-of-life that it constitutes.

Bearing in mind this redemptive project, each of the following chapters picks up a theme within traditional articulations of P4C and returns to it through a messianic lens. This means that the functional or operational aspects of Lipman's model have to be rendered inoperative in order to allow infancy to appear and new uses of language to be otherwise than an instrument of argumentative reasoning freed up. In short, we are not negating the origins of P4C. Instead we are living them differently, in suspension of Lipman's original goal-oriented formulation. For Lipman, "every educational enterprise, program, or project aims at some educational end."[39] Yet in the learning economy, it is precisely this claim that has put the philosophical dimension of his theory and practice at risk. The following book is not about critique so much as a redemption … but a redemption that only works in so far as P4C is put to a different, nonfunctional, noninstrumental use in the name of infancy.

Outline of the Chapters

Chapter 1: The Demand

We begin with a reconsideration of the quality of the speech offered by the P4C facilitator. To do so, we turn to a topic that has no visibility in the existing P4C literature: the question of the Voice of the teacher and the relationship of this Voice to the oath. It is our contention that overlooking the question of the Voice causes serious internal problems within the practice of P4C. Simply put, by Voice we refer to the unspeakable authority of the teacher that is never truly questioned (even in progressive, student-centered pedagogy) yet is the authority invested in the oaths that teachers and students take (to teach and to learn according to the laws of reason). Although never spoken as such, the Voice of the teacher is a perennial problem in progressive education. How much authority does it have? When and how should it intervene into a child's experience? Within the P4I community, the Voice of the teacher is rendered inoperative, the oath enacted only in order to suspend itself. This gesture does not negate the Voice of the teacher so much as maintains it in suspended animation so that the community can, in turn, experience the *demand* of the potentiality of language to be used without the supplement of the *command* of the Voice. The key to P4I is that the community ultimately forgets the Voice and, instead, can open itself up to respond to the demand of language to be spoken. The demand will thus emerge as the most important dimension of P4I. If Lipman argues that P4C concerns the cultivation of *reasonable* speech, then P4I concerns the exploration (not cultivation) of the *ontology* of speech (its demand). Or perhaps we can say that P4I is ontological speech, or speech that returns logic to its (disavowed and unacknowledged) origins in linguistic infancy (the ability to and not to speak).

Chapter 2: Rules

It is not uncommon for a community of inquiry to begin with members generating their own rules of discussion. The group decides what can and cannot be said and what kinds of speech acts constitute the community. Yet what is the nature of a "rule" and why are they so important for the practice of P4C? While the traditional literature on P4C emphasizes rules, it fails to theorize rules. To do so, we turn to Agamben and his distinction between rules (of a self-constituting community) and laws (that are imposed by authority from outside the community). On our interpretation of Agamben, rules are how a community responds to the demand of language (rather than the command of the teacher's Voice). They are how the community uses itself to investigate its own infancy in relation to the demand of language. Such rules do not stand over and above life (like laws that judge life) but are rather immanent to life as a form of self-instantiation or self-cultivation. While the law binds individuals to an abstract, universal order, rules bind us to each other, to a common life that emerges through infantile speech (speech that does not know what it is, who it is, how it is, but that it is). In P4I, rules are not imposed from the outside by the Voice of the teacher. Instead, they are generated by and through inquiry into the nature of the community itself and its own potentiality to speak.

Chapter 3: Adventure

With the suspension of the teacher's Voice and the emergent rules of its auto-constitution, the community of infancy can begin the adventure of thinking. While it is not uncommon to think of having an experience and then talking about it as following one another in a chronological sequence, for Agamben, the strange and paradoxical nature of an adventure is first and foremost a state of suspension in this causal relation, meaning that in an adventure the experience and the telling of that experience coincide without remainder. There is no ability to tell the difference between the event in its happening and the speaking of that event. A sense of adventure is only possible when and where there is a coincidence between what is happening and the telling of that happening, or an indeterminacy between act and speech. This kind of contact is best illustrated in the adventure of P4I where the event of feeling one's potentiality to speak coincides perfectly with the dialogue itself. At stake here is defining the unique phenomenological experience of speech in P4I as opposed to other kinds of speech in classrooms where speech is only offered up *after the fact* of learning or as *testimony to* a skill or disposition to come. As such, the qualities of speech in P4I differ from three common functions of speech in classrooms, including (a) confirmation of work completed, (b) explanation of possible wrongdoing, or (c) illustration of learning. Confirmation, explanation, and illustration separate speech from event whereas P4I allows us to rekindle this contact, thus infusing education with a sense of adventure.

Chapter 4: Love

Agamben also connects adventure with love, where the story of lovers coincides with the event of their love. Taking this observation up as a point of departure, we will theorize the centrality of love in P4I. Educational theorists have theorized love as an essential factor in education. Whereas, typically, a particular kind of love (erotic love, caring love, etc.) is argued to be especially relevant for educational practice, in this chapter we look at kinds of love that are constitutive for the contact between teacher and student. Specifically, we outline three types of love that one might find in a classroom. We argue that from the perspective of Agamben, the first two are problematic as they are not attentive to the potentiality of the student to be whatever and thus sacrifice potentiality of the child as such in the name of what must be (destiny) or what is (socialization). The third type of love, on the other hand, embraces the potentiality of the child. As an alternative to either "we are what we become" (destiny) or "we are what we are" (socialization), Agamben would call for another kind of love that recognizes whatever we are in the manner of our speaking (our infancy). This excess never corresponds to the *identity* we are supposed to assume (according to a destiny or to socialization). P4I cultivates love of whatever being through babble, which expresses the demand of language through modal oscillations (manners as a form of self-movement and self-modification). Whereas PC4 emphasizes learning logical skills (for the purpose of a rationally democratic life to come), P4I emphasizes the mannerisms of speaking that are ontological, meaning that they are the peculiar ways in which infancy erupts into every speech act as a reminder of the remainder of that which has not been said (the potentiality to speak). The former is love of destiny (as a predetermined telos) whereas the latter is love of whatever (as an infancy that exists right now in the mannerisms that emerge when the demand of language is genuinely felt). As such, P4I has its own, distinctive take on love in the classroom that differentiates it from other forms of love.

Chapter 5: Happiness

In most progressive and critical forms of pedagogy, the dominant affect that supports educational endeavors is hope: hope that students will live up to their potentials, hope that schools will transform society, hope that education will transform one's life. In this chapter, we want to argue for a hopeless education. But this is not at all a negative or nihilistic position. Instead we want to replace hope with joy and happiness in the actual act of being with students in a community of infancy. When involved in P4I, it is the immediate experience of potentiality that is inspirational. In this sense, joy and happiness are not future oriented. Nor are they critical. They are spontaneous expressions of what Agamben refers to as a form-of-life or a life that is not separated from its potentiality—an infantile life that fully assumes whatever it is. The problem with hope is that it always projects happiness and joy into the future and thus separates education (as preparation for something to be actualized in a future state) from potentiality as such. Only when we abandon hope can we find a new happiness in the now of collective potentialization.

Chapter 6: Anarchy

We will end this book with one final point of contact between P4I and politics. There seem to be two paradigms for thinking about politics and education. First, there is the instrumental approach that reduces education to the means to an externally defined political end. Liberal educational theory is symptomatic of this (i.e., education as preparation for democratic life). The worry with this paradigm is that education will lose its *educational* value and become nothing more than a tool for creating a political community. Second, there is the noninstrumental approach that asserts the autonomy of education from politics. While addressing the issue of instrumentalization, in fully separating education from politics, it nevertheless produces another problem: the reduction of education to a pure end in itself. Using Agamben as a point of departure, we would like to suggest that we need to rethink education (and P4I more specifically) as a pure means. To make this argument, we put forward the following theses. First, P4I is, at its base, an occupation of educational infrastructure (the space of the classroom and the time of learning) that suspends the function of this infrastructure. Second, such activity becomes political when the occupation of infrastructure is made into a public issue. Third, the politics that arises from this occupation is troubling and disconcerting because it is a noninstrumental politics that cannot be reduced to a set of clearly defined goals or objectives. This is a politics that is not about bringing a new society into existence so much as living this society *as not* this society, or this society in its potentiality to be otherwise than what it is. As such, there are no commands for a new kind of state or a new kind of constitution. Another way of saying this would be that there is no Voice that can be pinpointed as the guarantor of a particular kind of political speech. An example is the studious nature of Tiananmen Square. What is at stake in this chapter is defining occupation as the zone of contact between P4I and politics that displaces both: P4I becomes a public issue and politics loses its instrumental ends, becoming educational. The failure to think politics and education has thus far been the result of trying to think the two in relation. For us, making public the occupation of infrastructure is precisely the point of contact between education and politics that displaces where P4I can happen and who can participate while at the same time revealing a new, noninstrumental politics that does not know what it is or where it is going, and is therefore happy in so far as it does not have hope in the future. This hopelessness lends itself to experimentation with language and life right now, in the present, without waiting and without pause. In conclusion, the contact between P4I and politics produces a purely affirmative, infantile, common, precritical understanding of political life. Another name for this point of contact is none other than anarchy.

We can summarize the book as follows:

1. Ontology: Demand and Infancy
2. Social ontology: Rules
3. Aesthetics: Adventure
4. Ethics: Love and Happiness
5. Politics: Anarchy

Together, these chapters offer a redemption of P4C against the learning society, thus preserving what is most philosophical in the original practice: the experience of the demand of language through infantile speech. Paradoxically, such redemption does not happen through a continuance of the work of P4C nor its negation (post-Lipman style). Instead, redemption works only through rendering inoperative (neutralizing) the work of P4C in the form of P4I. As we will demonstrate, Agamben's method of philosophical analysis and his many concepts are helpful in deactivating discourses so that they can be studied. This means that at many points the voices of the authors and the voice of Agamben will fade in and out of one another. But such indistinction does not mean that the following book is merely an application of Agamben's thought. Indeed, the resulting form of educational life we explore helps to develop Agamben's project by grounding his comments on study, studious play, and contemplation in a *collective*, educational practice, and by redeeming his own notion of infancy (a concept that he has not, up till now, developed) as critical to an ontological account of the demand of language. Thus the first movement is an unworking of what works in P4C (to promote learning) and the second is a reworking of what is unworking in the work of Agamben (the lack of a collective educational practice through the abandoned concept of infancy in his early writings). This book is a contact between the two movements.

1

Demand

From the Sacred to the Profane

For critical theorist Ivan Illich, institutionalized schooling acts like a modernized, secular church, full of rituals and mystical incantations that have little to do with actual education and everything to do with preserving the sanctity of this most cherished institution through testing, accreditation, and graduation ceremonies. Illich writes, "The school system today performs the threefold function common to powerful churches throughout history. It is simultaneously the repository of society's myth, the institutionalization of that myth's contradictions, and the locus of the ritual, which reproduces and veils the disparities between myth and reality."[1] For Illich the school, with its hidden curriculum, becomes an institution of mystification, a ritual performance whose outcome is addiction to compulsive teaching and thus passive submission to an external authority—the teacher—who acts as a "priest" looking out for the flock. The net result: "School makes alienation preparatory to life, thus depriving education of reality and work of creativity. School prepares for the alienating institutionalization of life by teaching the need to be taught."[2] Stated differently, the major effect of schooling is the "progressive underdevelopment of self- and community-reliance."[3] Education is therefore no longer immanent to the self-regulation of the community by itself but rather a transcendental power to save a community from itself. Jan Masschelein and Maarten Simons add another important dimension to this argument.[4] For them, schools function as a form of secular baptism that offers children a *logos* or orientation for entering a specific world. For Masschelein and Simons, baptism leaves no room for the natality of newcomers, and in a sense, predetermines the course of an educational life. Although differing in terms of specific "recommendations," Illich and Masschelein and Simons argue that the function of the teacher as priest ("sacrament of teaching") and of schooling as baptism ("sacrament of learning") need to be suspended in order for new forms of educational life to be possible. And it is important to point out that the theological language deployed by these theorists is not merely metaphorical. Instead, it points toward a disavowed origin of the school, an ecclesiastical apparatus that has yet to be fully acknowledged.

In what follows, we will further this line of inquiry by focusing explicitly on the role of the teacher's Voice and of the oath in giving body to such sacraments. To do so, we will turn to the work of Agamben that, like those of Illich and Masschelein and Simons, concerns the entanglement of secular institutions with theological and economic discourses and practices. While Illich and Masschelein emphasize the ecclesiastical underpinnings of institutional forms (and the school in particular), Agamben turns toward the question of language and Voice, thus further developing the significance of Illich and Masschelein and Simons's work. For instance, in his book *The Sacrament of Language: An Archeology of the Oath*, Agamben analyzes the oath in order to understand the very origins and function of language.[5] He states that the oath is "the historical testimony of the experience of language in which man [sic] was constituted as a speaking being."[6] To show how Agamben's exploration of the function of oath is relevant to education, we will (1) explain how the historical significance of the oath (as a "sacrament of power") points to a more originary function, namely that of guaranteeing the truthfulness of language ("sacrament of language"), and why Agamben believes that the oath needs to be made inoperable through the work of philosophy. (2) As it is in the juridical, religious, political realms, the oath is an apparatus of the Voice (in this case, the Voice of the teacher as priest). (3) Lastly, we show how such operability can be suspended by building on what Agamben says about the role of philosophy and connecting it with the practice of P4I. It is our contention that the community of infancy can make the oath inoperable by silencing the Voice of the teacher. Again drawing on Agamben, we can describe this as a form of profanation (as opposed to secularization) in that it frees language from the sacred use in the oath and makes it available for new and different use, returning schooling to its original meaning as "free time"[7] and thereby making possible new, profane forms of educational life beyond the teacher as priest and schooling as baptism. Along the way, we will redefine the role of the facilitator in the P4I community: no longer someone who blesses or curses but rather opens up a space and time for the demand of language to be felt by the community. In this sense, oath taking and making guaranteed by the authority of the Voice of the teacher are replaced with a more originary or infantile experience of the demand of language as such. The surprising upshot of this argument is that the teacher as priest is replaced by the teacher-as-not-teacher or teacher as clown with the job of profaning the sacredness of his or her Voice so that the demand of language from within the community itself can be heard.

This problematic of the oath and Voice might sound unfamiliar to those within the P4C community. More often then not, the question of the relationship between teachers and students is cast in terms of a dialectic between teacher authority and student interests. For instance, Olivier Michaud and Riku Välitalo argue that two extremes are to be avoided in P4C: traditional authority and anarchy. In the first instance, the teacher is in authority in the classroom by holding power over students as an authority figure, and in the second, the teacher abnegates such authority, allowing students maximum freedom to pursue their interests. Rejecting both options, the authors argue for a new notion of democratically constructed and shared authority in which authority is not a mere possession of the teacher nor is it rejected. Instead, authority is judiciously employed to structure the classroom so that students can "make decisions, express their opinions, follow their interests"[8] without any of these being dictated in advance by the teacher's authority. While we are sympathetic with this project, we would like to offer several revisions. First, we want to focus on the level of language and the ontology of language (infancy). To do so, we have to reposition the problem of "relationality" to the linguistic level of oath making and oath taking. Without this move, we fear that attempts to rethink authority will not actually escape the gravitational pull of the ecclesiastical origins of the school and of teaching as outlined above. On our reading, the only way out of a reinscription of the sacredness of education is a turn toward infantile speech (as speech that does not respond to a command from the authority of the Voice to take an oath so much as to a demand of language). Second, as will be addressed in the final chapter of this book, the privileging of democracy as a teleological destiny toward which the community ought to be directed is, on our reading, somewhat premature and actually obscures the more primary philosophical experience of the demand of infancy, which, in the last analysis, is anarchic. Instead of a democratic horizon offering salvation (through the blessed speech of reasonableness), what is at stake is the profane and common experience of the demand of infancy as a point of contact between teacher and student.

The Voice

At the heart of the philosophical enterprise rests the problem of the Voice and how the Voice always casts philosophy in relation to negation and destiny. In this section, we will outline this problem of Voice and then articulate it in relation to Agamben's thoughts on the oath. For us, the experience of infancy can only happen when Voice and oath are rendered inoperative, creating a clearing for a positive experience of the potentiality for speaking (infancy).

In *Language and Death: The Place of Negativity*, Agamben takes pains to demonstrate the intricate relationship between philosophical thinking and negation via the Voice. Referencing Hegel and Heidegger as paradigms of metaphysical speculation in Western philosophy, Agamben finds in both a reliance on an ineffable and unsayable Voice as the foundation for the human experience of being in language. With reference to Heidegger, the problem is as follows. Animals have a natural voice that they spontaneously express (the call of birds, the chirping of crickets). Humans, on the other hand, have language that must be learned. Their language does not belong to them but must be inherited or transmitted. Because humans only have language, there is an essential gap or lack that defines their linguistic experience. There is *no necessary link* between language and voice in human experience. Between the two is only silence or a basic sense of negativity. From inside this negativity, Heidegger posits the Voice of conscience as an existential foundation. Such a Voice is not a vocalization. It has no content of its own. Instead it is a silent call. Agamben summarizes, "[W]ithout a voice in the place of language, Dasein [Heidegger's name for human beings] finds *another Voice*, even if this is a Voice that calls only in the mode of silence."[9] Thus, we find in our human experience of language a double negation: the negation of the animal voice for language and the silent negation of the Voice of conscience (which is ineffable, lacking content of its own). On Agamben's interpretation, "the experience of Being is the experience of a Voice that calls without saying anything, and human thought and words are born merely as an 'echo' of this Voice."[10] This opens a division in human experience defined by an essential negativity: on the one hand is the silent speech of the Voice of Being that, because of its silence, can never be spoken by human words; on the other hand is the world of human utterances as an echo of this unspoken and ultimately disavowed ground. The upshot of this Heideggerian interpretation of the relation between humans and language is that "discourse cannot speak its taking place"[11] because its origin lies outside of itself in the eternal mystery of the Voice.

Poetry, for Agamben, likewise is stuck in the metaphysics of negativity. Instead of the Voice of conscience, we find the Voice of the Muses as a stand-in for the ungraspability or unspeakability of the event of language. In the metrical-musical structure of poetry, the poem is caught in the negative sway of memory and repetition that always misses its taking place. Muses step in to fill the void of this taking place as an external, mystical supplement. But because Muses are ineffable, the ground of poetic utterance remains within the negative register. Yet Agamben's careful analysis of the poem *L'infinito* by Giacomo Leopardi suggests that poetry, when it attempts to rigorously study its own form, can offer up a way out of this negativity. The last line of the poem gestures back to the first in the form of "sweet drowning." While drowning may appear to be another manifestation of an essential negativity, the negativity is positively redeemed as "sweet." What makes it sweet is a unification of the time of the poem in its utterance—a time that does not need Muses any longer but finds its own taking place sufficient for its grounding. In short, the poem ends with a return to its beginning. But this return is not a dialectical sublation nor is it simply a return to the same. Instead, the return is the shortest of journeys that *affirms* (rather than negates) its own event, its own potentiality for taking place. As Agamben summarizes, "[I]n this voyage the experience of the event of the word which opened its unheard silence and interminable spaces in thought, ceases to be a negative experience."[12] Nietzsche also gestures toward a post-philosophy of the "last man" who no longer hears any Voice or Muse and is thus abandoned to his relationship with language as such. "Thought," writes Agamben about Nietzsche,

> after the end of philosophy cannot still be thought of the Voice, of the taking place of language in the Voice; nor can it be the thought of the death of the Voice [as that would merely reinsert negativity back into our relation with language]. Only if the human voice is not simply death but has never existed, only if language no longer refers to any Voice (and, thus, not even to a *gramma*, that is, to a removed voice), is it possible for man [sic] to experience a language that is not marked by negativity and death.[13]

When placed side by side, the philosophical poetry of Leopardi and the poetic philosophy of Nietzsche open up the possibility for thinking language freed from negativity: language in *infancy*. But before we elaborate on a positive experience of infancy through philosophical dialogue, let us turn briefly to destiny.

Negation is intimately connected with the problem of destiny. Destiny throws us into a particular tradition and language. It condemns us to a certain fate. But where does this destiny come from? Again, we find it in our inner Voice. In philosophy, Agamben argues that later Heidegger attempts to free Voice from negativity via the concept of *Ereignis* or event. Yet it does not seem that *Ereignis* is capable of this maneuver. Agamben summarizes his critique as follows: "In *Ereignis*, we might say, Voice shows itself as that which, remaining unsaid and unsignified in every word and in every historical tradition, consigns humanity to history and signification as the unspeakable tradition that forms the foundation for all tradition and human speech."[14] In other words, *Ereignis* does not suspend negativity; it merely conceals it as the unnamed that destines humanity to a particular tradition and language. Destiny is therefore linked to a sense of negativity (as an unsaid excess outside language as an eventual horizon of signification). We, as human beings, are destined by negativity to a particular tradition and language, and this destiny is outside of the very traditions and languages that we have at hand to theorize, resist, or transform such destiny. Heidegger's only response to this problem is that humans as mortals must await the arrival of new gods.

From Voice to Oath

At this point, we can pivot to Agamben's theory of the oath. It is our contention that the oath is the way in which language can make operative the silence of the Voice. It is, in this sense, the *linguistic apparatus* of the Voice. And for this reason, the oath is an accomplice in destining humanity to its tradition and language (whatever these might be). At the same time, as Agamben would say, we cannot simply negate the oath in order to liberate ourselves from such a destiny. Instead, as we will see, the "solution" to the problem is to discover infancy within the operativity of the oath, animating it from the inside. To do so, Agamben attempts to deactivate the oath (as a curse or a blessing). But this is more complex than it would at first appear, as the mere inoperativity of the oath itself is not enough to truly profane this apparatus of the Voice. Instead, what Agamben will call for is a more radical gesture: the inoperativity of the inoperativity of the oath. While this might seem rather paradoxical (let alone foreign to educational concerns), it is important to remember the problem at hand: How can discourse speak its own taking place? How can discourse be found in its own positive potentiality to be spoken (rather than in the negativity of the Voice)?

Simply stated, before the advent of either religious ritual or political institutions, the oath was a linguistic utterance that "confirm[ed] and guarantee[d]" the order of things (destined them).[15] Drawing on the linguist Benveniste's work on the oath, Agamben further defines its function as that which supports, guarantees, and demonstrates. The oath "I pledge," for instance, is a way of "guaranteeing the truth and efficacy of language."[16] Stated differently, the oath sutures together words and actions, language and world so that meaning is guaranteed, not unlike the work of the Voice. The Voice (of conscience) is precisely what steps in to reconcile nature and culture, voice and language, and thus to guarantee truth and meaning by providing speech with an unspeakable (and thus negative) ground outside of itself. Articulating the two, we argue that the Voice is the silent conscience behind the taking up of oaths (or what prompts the taking of the oath in the first place). On this reading, the oath is supported by but also conceals the negativity of the Voice.

The problem, as Agamben sees it, is that while the oath was created to prevent perjury, perjury is only a crime if the oath is presupposed. As such, perjury is *contained* within the very structure of the oath itself! In other words, even the person most faithful to the oath is still capable of an act of supreme perjury. But Agamben is quick to point out that this deficit is not merely a psychological critique of human beings who are incapable of keeping their word. Rather, Agamben argues that the fundamental fissure in the structure of the oath as containing within it both the potential of swearing and perjury indicates a "weakness pertaining to language itself"[17] wherein words can always refer to multiple things they were not intended to refer to. The sacredness of the oath is therefore also already a profanity of the very guarantee, efficacy, and certainty that the oath was an attempt to secure.

But this is not merely an obscure point of relevance only to historians. Agamben's archaeology of the oath reminds us that even this most archaic structure of the oath remains important for understanding language as such. As with all of Agamben's work, the "origin" does not exist in the past; it is internal to the present. This is a nonchronological understanding of origins—one that forces us to confront a threshold of indistinction between now and then, between our secular institutions and their ancient origins in the sacredness of ritual. According to Agamben, "the contemporary interest of an archeology of the oath" lies in the fact that "[u]ltrahistory, like anthropogenesis, is not in fact an event that can be considered completed once and for all; it is always under way, because *Homo Sapiens* never stops becoming man [*sic*], has perhaps not yet finished entering language and swearing to his nature as a speaking being."[18] In short, the origin is always already operative when we take a position in language. Thus, whenever we stake a claim (and thus swear an oath) we also open ourselves up to the possibility of perjury.

Another aspect of the oath that Agamben identifies is its relationship to the curse (*sacratio* can mean curse; *sacramentum* is one of the Latin terms for oath, in Greek, *ara* can mean curse or prayer). According to Agamben, the oath has been seen as a "conditional curse," insofar as "[t]o swear is first of all … to curse oneself in the event that one says what is false or does not do what has been promised."[19] In other words, the oath cannot be separated from its opposite, the curse. So there is not, first, the oath, then divine testimony, and then the curse. For instance, in ancient oaths, there is often expressed both a good omen and a bad omen so that the curse follows a blessing or vice versa. As an example, Agamben cites the following:

> To those who swear loyally and remain faithful to their own, may children give them joy, may the earth grant its products in abundance, may their herds be fruitful, and may they be filled with other blessings, them and their children; but to perjurers may the earth not be productive nor their herds fruitful; may they perish terribly, them and their stock![20]

In this case, the blessing and the curse arrive together as co-originary possibilities within the oath. In short, curse and oath are epiphenomena of "one sole experience of language"[21] as a kind of undivided unity of opposites, as a potentiality for saying this and saying that, of swearing this and perjuring that, of blessing this and cursing that. When one risks one's self in the act of speaking, one therefore exposes the self to both truth and lying. The oath, which was supposed to guarantee the connection between word and action, language and world, is an unstable fault line that profanes itself in its most basic operations. Stated differently, the necessity of the oath gives way to the contingencies of language. The oath, as a linguistic apparatus of the Voice, cannot uphold the destiny of humans precisely because it has within it incompatible opposites that *un-destine* one another.

Blasphemy is then the symmetrical other to the sacred use of language in the oath. Whereas in the oath, the name of God guarantees the connection between words and actions ("In the name of God, I swear that I will ... "), in the act of blasphemy the efficacy of the name is cursed. Like perjury, blasphemy separates words from deeds/things. Summarizing, Agamben writes, "The name of God, released from the signifying connection, becomes blasphemy, vain and meaningless speech, which precisely through this divorce from meaning becomes available for improper and evil uses."[22] The undivided experience of language that we have in the oath is therefore split. The sole experience of language is lost when blasphemy takes precedence.

The contemporary result of this archeology of the oath throughout Western history is a coterminous splitting of language into logic and science on one side as pure management of statements and, on the other side, religion, art, and poetry as signifying surpluses. What is lost in both cases is an experience of language as potentially *both* truth and error, blessing and curse *together before the split* without negation and without destiny. This would be a purely affirmative experience that says "yes" to the infancy of language as a pure potentiality to speak. Once split like this, language in its infancy—its potentiality uncoupled from negativity and destiny—can no longer be thought. Human language became possible when a living being

> found itself co-originarily exposed to the possibility of both truth and lie, committed itself to respond with its life for its words, to testify in the first person for them. ... so also does the oath express the demand, decisive in every sense for the speaking animal, to put its nature at stake in language and to bind together in an ethical and political connection words, things, and actions. Only by this means was it possible for something like a history, distinct from nature and, nevertheless, inseparably intertwined with it, to be produced.[23]

When the vanity of speech eclipses the oath, then human life as such is put in jeopardy—a radical nihilism opens up in the very heart of our relationship to language. This nihilism is the ultimate cost of the negativity of the Voice made fully manifest.

The problem today is that the efficacy of the oath as a performative speech act is in a constitutive crisis, and the resulting nihilism spreads throughout cultural and educational forms of life. When the co-originary structure of the oath is split from its internal relationship to the curse, then we have a split in the very life of the human experiment. On the one hand, we see ongoing examples of the living being reduced to bare life (the voice of pain and suffering). In Agamben's work,[24] this is illustrated by a number of contemporary figures ranging from prisoners in concentration camps, to refugees, to coma patients. In all cases, there is a fissure that opens between survival and language. Bare life is a kind of invisible life, whose voice is mere *pathos*, lacking a *logos* that would make it relevant/intelligible to those who have a certain power or privilege to respond. On the other hand, we find the speaking being whose words are increasingly devoid of meaning or relevance. Here we find the sound bite, the slogan, or the circulation of amusing internet memes replacing the possibility of experiencing one's self through the efficacy and truthfulness of giving one's word. This condition might be referred to as communicative capitalism or a capitalism that capitalizes on the circulation of continual speech through social media and communication technologies.[25] Speech in this sense becomes absorbed into a spectacle. If industrial capitalism operated through the expropriation of labor power (work), now it expropriates symbolic power (communication). Agamben summarizes,

This means that a fuller Marxian analysis should deal with the fact that capitalism (or any other name one wants to give the process that today dominates world history) was directed not only toward the expropriation of productive activity, but also and principally toward the alienation of language itself, of the very linguistic and communicative nature of humans, of that *logos* which one of Heraclitus's fragments identified as the Common.[26]

The results are as superficial as they are nihilistic: a playland of communication that is vacuous and incessant.

In short, the oath in contemporary society is largely inoperative. But this does not mean that Agamben calls for a mere return to the operativity of the oath as a solution to such problems as outlined above. Not only would this be simple nostalgia, but even worse, it would miss the central point of his archeology of the oath: that the preconditions for our current situation are internal to the very structure of the oath itself. Stated differently, we do not need new ritual baptisms so as to secure life and word, word and action. At the same time, to question the primacy of the oath, Agamben does not wish to abolish, negate, or destroy it. Rather, Agamben's strategy to break with the dialectic of blessing and curse, swearing and perjury is to suspend the suspension, to render inoperative the inoperativity of the oath in today's society. This is not a negation of a negation, but rather the suspension of the suspension of the linguistic apparatus (the inoperative oath) of a negation (the Voice) in the name of an un-destined form of life.

The means to enact this elaborate strategy can be found in philosophy (or at least a specific kind of poetic philosophy or infantile philosophy). At its heart, philosophy, according to Agamben, is precisely that which pronounces "yes" to language without swearing or cursing, without abiding in either truth or error, the sacred or the blasphemous. "Philosophy is," Agamben summarizes, "constitutively a critique of the oath: that is, it puts in question the sacramental bond that links the human being to language, without for that reason simply speaking haphazardly, falling into the vanity of speech."[27] Agamben's philosophical archeology of the oath thus has three movements to it. First, there is a speculative history that charts the operability of the oath and its constitutive aporias. Second, it pinpoints how the present moment has rendered the oath inoperative by splitting the word from action/life/things (the predominance of blasphemy). Third, he suggests that the role of philosophy is not to repair the oath and make it operable again, but rather to render inoperative that which is inoperative, to render indifferent that which has become indifferent. This is a kind of second-order level of indifference that, in turn, offers a "line of resistance and change."[28] Thus the nihilism of spectacle and the expropriation of language become a "positive possibility"[29] to be used against this very condition. It is only when we let idle the oath and blasphemy, blessing and curse that philosophy can once again give us the experience of language as such without recourse to the negativity of the Voice. This would be a positive experience of the infancy of language.

From Taking an Oath to Responding to a Demand (of Language) in P4I

Now, we can return to our opening comments concerning education and its relation to the sacrament of baptism. Baptism is a sacrament, and a sacrament is a kind of oath. For Agamben, both ancient sources and most scholars agree that the oath should be seen as a form of *sacratio*. He refers, for example, to Festus, who writes that "[o]ne calls '*sacramentum*' (one of the two Latin terms for oath) ... an act that is done with the sanction of the oath," and to Benveniste, who observes that "the term *sacramentum* ... implies the notion of making '*sacer*'."[30] According to what has been said before (Illich, Masschelein, and Simons), students in the typical classroom are being baptized by the teacher. The teacher is *sanctifying* (officiating/administrating/presiding over) the oath by speaking with a certain Voice and expecting the students to do the same ("Repeat after me: ... "). It is the students who actually *take* the oath (receive the sacrament/baptism) by repeating after the teacher, that is, by echoing the Voice of the teacher. But because, as we have seen, every oath contains an acceptance of the consequences should one fail to fulfill the pledge, the students are actually cursing *themselves* as they are performing the oath. Thus, they repeat the essential negativity of the Voice (of the teacher), this time directed at themselves at the precise moment they swear an oath to repeat.

The contemporary crisis in teaching is really a crisis in the structure of this oath. In this sense, we part ways somewhat with Illich and Masschelein and Simons. Instead of seeing the school and the teacher as sacred and education as a sacrament, we feel that the contemporary manifestation of the school, like most institutions, is dominated by blasphemy against the sacred. Standardization has split the Voice of the teacher from their word, resulting in a situation where the teacher can no longer stake their lives in the performance of their word (hence the teacher is no longer a priest or judge but rather a bureaucrat). There is no Voice of conscience underlying the teacher's language, granting it a destiny. The "teacher" is merely a functionary position within the bureaucratic management of learning. Teaching as a form of educational life has been rendered inoperative precisely by standardization, which makes teaching an empty form of life for the teacher. Whereas the oath once offered a linguistic space where one could stake one's life (find one's destiny), now the language of teaching is merely superficial ("Just take the test, don't ask me what it means") or blasphemous ("This is just a job, so I don't have to give a damn").

But this does not mean that we are calling for a return to the oath in order to save the profession of the teacher. Such a move, as outlined above, would only be a nostalgic fantasy that does not face the aporia of the oath itself. Hence a possible inadequacy in progressive and radical calls for a return to the autonomy of the teacher and an appeal to their conscience: without a problematization of the Voice of the teacher, the oath is simply reinstated without recognizing how the Voice always already indicates the sacred (and hence sacrificial) as negation and destiny.

So to suspend the suspension of the Voice of the teacher, they have to abandon the oath (sacred speech) and blasphemy (vain speech), that is, in some way make inoperative the constitutive relation and subsequent non-relation between praising and cursing. This would mean that the Voice of the teacher no longer speaks the language of true and false without falling into mere haphazard nonsense either. But what is left when teachers no longer swear or curse at their students? What is left when the teacher has no Voice? Here, we suggest one alternative is to theorize the relation between teaching and silence, or, at least, the silencing of the silence of the Voice of the teacher. By this, we do not mean lack of language or lack of speaking, but rather the suspension of the Voice that renders language a game of oath taking, of blessing or cursing.

One attempt to do so might be P4C. In the classic model of P4C, the teacher is a mere facilitator of the community of inquiry. For example, when discussing the use of the philosophical novel in the classroom for jumpstarting community of inquiry, Lipman makes the following observation concerning the role of the teacher (or lack thereof):

> But if the model is a novel, what happens to the live teaching in the actual classroom—isn't he or she supposed to be the model of thinking for the live pupils, and of thinking about thinking and all those other good things as well? My own opinion is that classroom teachers have seldom been in a position to provide their pupils with a model of inquiry into inquiry or learning to learn, nor is it essential that they think they need to be in such a position. The responsibility for such modeling can be appropriately delegated to the novel and the classroom community of inquiry.[31]

Lipman downplays the role of the teacher in fostering a community of inquiry. Another way of stating this is that he is rejecting both the traditional authority of the teacher and anarchy in favor of a shared authority. Shared authority is mediated through the novels themselves. As such, Lipman is keen to silence the Voice of the teacher, and by extension, the teacher's authority no longer commands oath taking by students. This is certainly true, and a valuable attempt to separate the position of the teacher from that of the sacred role of the one who baptizes. At the same time, it is important to note that the Voice has not disappeared; it has merely been displaced into the novel, which now speaks *on behalf of the teacher*. The teacher is no longer a teacher with a Voice because the book has assumed this role. The Voice ventriloquizes through the novel, which embodies the sacredness of a certain kind of language and discourse "blessed" by the laws of reasonableness traditionally enforced by the teacher. Or, perhaps even more interestingly, Lipman's observation that other children in the community will act as a model of normative behavior does not seem to solve the question of the Voice either. Instead, the normative authority of the novel's Voice is merely taken on by the community itself through slow habituation. In both cases, the children in the community must take an *oath* to the model of the novel or of exemplary behavior of members of the group that are most reasonable in their responses in order to be baptized into a deliberative democratic community. The children therefore *respond* to a command "repeat after me" that constitutes their identity within the community through an oath. But to do so repeats the aporia of the oath that is always already a curse.

In sum, Lipman's fundamental critique is correct. He is asking us to think the speaking of the P4C facilitator beyond swearing ("This is the right answer!" Or: "Listen to me because I know what I am talking about") or cursing ("Don't say that, it is not allowed"). This would also be an experience of the teacher's speech without therefore turning it into blasphemous or meaningless speech ("You should do it because I TOLD YOU SO!" or "Say whatever you want, there is no truth, no justice … it's all the same to me!"). Yet the sacrament of language and the ritual of baptism into a community of inquiry are not problematized enough in Lipman's comments. Indeed, they are implicitly smuggled back into the secular, liberal model as "solutions" to the rise in dominance of blasphemous speech.

Are we thus trapped? Or is there a way to *profane the speech of the teacher* in such a way that does not simply displace the problematic of the Voice and the oath? Is there an experience and experiment with language that does not bless or curse in the classroom but is purely an affirmation of language (a saying "yes" to infancy)? It is our contention that P4I can do so, silencing the Voice of the teacher without displacement, thus effectively neutralizing the problematic of the oath in relation to an educational practice. To give a simple illustration, the teacher speaks without a Voice when he or she whispers: "Repeat after me, I do not know how to talk but I cannot not speak!" Notice that this is radically different from the typical understanding of shared authority. Shared authority, as it is conceptualized in P4C, means that the teacher states, "Repeat after me, I do not know what I am saying" and thus models fallibility and epistemological humility. Yet while this teacher might not know what they are saying, he or she still knows how to speak (according to the laws of reasonableness to which an oath has been taken). This position is best summarized by Maughn Rollins Gregory who writes that the P4C facilitator "isn't teaching *what* to think, but *how* to think [and] exchanges content expertise for procedural expertise."[32] Renouncing certainty for fallibility does not render inoperative the apparatus of the oath, as the facilitator has still pledged themselves to a certain procedure for which they are held responsible. This, in turn, allows the facilitator to "bless" certain philosophical moves (rather than positions) made by students so that they can remain on the path toward reasonableness (as a telos of deliberative, communal inquiry).

"Repeat after me, I do not know how to talk but I cannot not speak!" not only suspends the oaths associated with how and what to speak. It also *positively* expresses *that* one can speak. It is a response to a certain demand (as we will see below) that one speak, full stop. There is no destiny orienting this speech nor is there any way to bless or curse it. Instead, there is only the affirmation of a certain arrival of speech that cannot not be spoken (that demands to be spoken). The teacher-as-not-a-teacher does not make or command an oath to this appearance of speech. Rather he or she simply testifies to its occurrence, carving out a space and a time in the classroom where speaking *can be noticed at its point of infancy* (before it is routed toward what and how to speak). Pointing toward one's own conditions of speaking does not collapse the position of the teaching to that of the student, as students barely notice *that* they speak. Instead, they are most often oriented toward what to say and how to say it, as these are the dimensions of speaking that are privileged by the laws of learning.

But what if the students decide to stay quiet, fall silent (following the lead of the teacher to actually be silent—as one option)? Put differently, what makes them want to break their silence and talk at all? If there is no model to guide the speaking, and if there is no oath to hold participants accountable to this model, then what drives the inquiry? Classically, it is student interests that hold open the place of inquiry. Yet it is not clear to us that this is actually what happens when teachers do philosophy with children. Think here of a simple situation in which a rather strange question is proposed—one that is decisively out of the ordinary, abstract, or downright weird to students (such as "what is time?"). This question might not be of any compelling interest to students, yet suddenly the question takes off, and students become impassioned. They feel a certain pressure to speak and sometimes cannot constrain themselves from speaking (sitting on hands or inflating cheeks only lasts for so long). Intervening in the ensuring dialogue by a teacher exerting their Voice might interrupt the flow, causing the pressure to speak to dissipate. What might be sacrificed is precisely the urgency that one cannot not speak in such a moment. It is this pressure for speech to speak itself without guarantees, in its infancy, that is negated when a greater lesson in reasonability takes precedence, commanding an oath to a certain procedure of inquiry that preexists the event of speaking. "I *must* speak even though it probably doesn't make sense and I don't know exactly what I am about to say!" The urgency of infancy expresses itself as an impotentiality: the student simply cannot *not* bear to speak; they are suddenly bursting at the seams with the overriding sensation of *speakability* or infancy. Just as such urgency cannot be commanded by a Voice of the teacher's authority (which interrupts infancy by pausing to reaffirm an oath), it is equally inadequate to describe it in terms of student interests. Interests might emerge out of the dialogue, they might be produced by the community, but this can only happen insofar as the common demand of infancy is taken up in the first place.

At this point, we take recourse to Agamben's notion of the *demand* (the original Italian, *esigenza*, can also be mean necessity, urgency, or need). There is a demand at the heart of P4I (not a command to take an oath). But this demand does not come from the teacher or from following interests. Notice a shift: the teacher does not administer/command an oath or simply allow students to speak about whatever they are interested in but rather allows for a demand to be exposed through testifying to one's infancy, which does not have recourse to the unspeakable authority of the Voice. As such, the demand does not contain within it the potential to curse or to bless (according to the authority of the Voice) but rather merely opens up (occurs/manifests itself in) a space where speaking can happen, or more aptly, where speaking can experience its own taking place in the constitution of a community. In other words, the operation at stake here is that the *ethical* dimension of oath taking is suspended in order to discover how a demand is more ontologically primary. It is what is in common that makes the community of infancy possible in its infancy (rather than for a specific destiny).

For Agamben, the demand is an ontological category (rather than merely a linguistic one, or rather, it demonstrates how language—infancy—is itself ontologically primordial). In other words, it highlights the necessary and sufficient condition underlying existence in general. The book *The Use of Bodies* charts the history of the demand from Spinoza's *conatus* (striving) to Leibniz's *vinculum substantiale* (substantial bond), uncovering an alternative to the ontology of substance and essence wherein existence is demand. Citing Agamben, "what the possible demands is not to pass to the act, but to materialize itself, to become matter."[33] The possible (or potential/infancy) *demands* that it materialize itself *now*, not through negation of what is or through the actualization of a destiny, but as the affirmative repotentialization of what is. All substance responds to the demand and, in so doing, expresses an impotentiality (an ability to not *not* be). This is not a command issued from an external source nor is it an interest (as interests already assert the existence of the subject who has interests). Weirdly, this demand is impersonal and disinterested insofar as it preexists the arrival of subjects with specific characteristics and interests defining them as "individuals." It is rather an ontological pressure to strive. Stated differently, existence is its own *immanent cause* (necessity), its own patient and agent, cause and effect, potentiality and act. Matter *exposes* its immanent cause when it does not negate itself but shows itself in its potentiality. Instead of overcoming itself (through negation), existence must become itself through an impotent response to the demand to become. The same applies to speaking. The infancy of speech (speakability) demands to be spoken in such a way that it does not exhaust its infancy but rather continually repotentializes itself in relation to this infancy.

As Agamben states, "[I]n demand, things are contemplated."[34] Contemplation is not concerned with the problematic of reasonableness so much as with ontological questions or the logic of existence. Hence the charge of P4I is not to teach skills or dispositions or civic virtues so much as to return to the most basic ontological experience: the demand of infancy for infantile speech (or speech that exposes its own impotentiality to not *not* be spoken). The demand turns us toward this sayability and thus provides space for contemplation, and contemplation repotentializes what is sayable in the demand, producing an immanent relation of cause and effect.

Applying this to P4I—as a practice of contemplating the sayable and saying the contemplatable—we can now offer a number of conclusions. In responding to the demand of language, the community speaks its own taking place and therefore assumes its own infancy as a positive condition of its striving. The demand is the immanent cause of the community as it feels the necessity to constitute itself out of itself, using the only medium at its disposal: language. Given this structure of the demand, the community is equally passive and active in that participants respond to a demand that their very interaction makes possible in the first place. On this interpretation, the silencing of the teacher's Voice is not so participants can listen to each other's interests and cultivate reasonableness through deliberative evaluations and judgments according to the oath that has been taken. Instead, in P4I, the idea is to listen to the impersonal and disinterested demand of language as such. The P4I circle is therefore not just the circulation of reasoned viewpoints on a topic of shared interest but rather a space for a demand to be experienced and experimented with without knowing how the experiment will go or how it should go or where it should go. In sum, if P4C emphasizes logical talk, P4I emphasizes ontological talk, or talk that hits upon and responds to the demands of language as such.

Again, while this might all seem rather abstract, it actually describes a very real phenomenon for anyone who has facilitated a P4I session: Children feel compelled to respond to a demand that is not reducible to their interests or desires. There is an excitement in being *taken up* or *carried away* by a demand that one does not fully understand or comprehend but nevertheless is compelling. And if this sounds overly passive, the key point is that the community itself, through dialogue, is the agent that carries itself away from itself! This demand calls forth language in its infancy, as an experiment in speaking that constitutes the self and the community without recourse to negation (of the unreasonable for the reasonable) or any telos or destiny (as a guarantor of legitimate speech). Instead, there is only the loop between demand and contemplation that drives dialogue this way and that. The teacher exposes the demand that allows the students to speak, to repotentialize their speaking so that the infancy of speaking can materialize itself. In turn, the community responds to the demand through its own *use of itself* or its auto-affection in the form of rule generation (as will be explored in the next chapter). Rules on this interpretation are precisely the technique a community uses to carry itself away, to take itself up.

Here is but one example. During a P4I session with college students in a class titled "Inquiry and Dialogue in the Arts" one of us (Tyson) put up on the screen Magritte's famous painting *Ceci n'est pas une Pipe* (1929). No one showed any interest in the image whatsoever, and there was silence in the room. Finally Tyson asked, "What questions does this painting ask of us?" Notice how this question directed attention toward what the image demanded (not toward interests students might have in the image). The image was demanding several kinds of questions such as "what is an image?" or "what is a pipe?" or "are there not different kinds of pipes with degrees of 'reality'?" or "what makes something the kind of thing that it is anyway?" The students responded to these demands through dialogic contemplation, the source of which was nothing more than their capacity to speak (their collective infancy). And through the course of the dialogue, they started to formulate rules and procedures for answering these questions that were not dictated by any laws of reasonability predicated beforehand but rather by the seeming "irrationality" of the image itself (by and through their exposure to a demand). There was no Voice there to ensure a separation between blessed from cursed speech (and thus ensure a certain telos toward the correct procedure or the correct answer), and students did not take an oath to only speak "reasonably" (thereby prematurely cursing themselves in the process). They were taken up and carried away by the image—not *toward* a specific destination (as prescribed by the teacher's Voice), but rather *around* the questions the image demanded of them. As such, there was only the self-propelling striving (toward what, we don't know) of continually repotentializing the dialogue through the only resource at hand: the infancy of speech in relation to a demand placed upon the community by the image.

What Then of the Facilitator in the Community of Infancy?

> Dilan: There's a difference between time and how we keep track of time. Time is going on. Without time we would all be frozen, like one frame in a movie.
>
> Noopur: (Agrees.) There are scientific reasons for 24-hour day. In Egypt time is what balances life. Without time there would be series of events without stopping.

At this point a P4I facilitator feels compelled to intervene: "But Noopur, how could there be a 'series of events' without time? What do you think of Dilan's distinction between time and how we measure time? Does everybody agree that without time we would all be frozen?" This intervention would certainly appear reasonable, considering that it allows the facilitator to point out an apparent contradiction (series of events without time) and to identify an important distinction (two types/uses of time) that may otherwise go unnoticed. And indeed, if the primary goal is to improve students' thinking skills according to the ultimate criterion of reasonableness, the facilitator would need to intervene to ensure the movement toward the intended goal. The facilitator must make the question *function* in accordance with a certain telos (destiny). The teacher must sanctify the language of the students through a certain form of linguistic baptism. And yet there is a deep sense that this process is valuable in itself as an experience in and with language and that any kind of intervention would take away from the experience, leading students from language taking place to language as it is destined to become: rational, democratic discourse.

This is where the facilitator has to make a decision. It is the decision between inquiry and infancy. Intervention means continuing the ritual of teaching by reaffirming the Voice as the guarantor of reasonableness—stepping in from outside the dialogue to keep the dialogue on track, maintain its course onward toward its destiny in reasonableness and fair judgment. Only if the teacher opts not to intervene (as a priest, blessing the process), becomes *in-fans*, as it were, can they keep open the experience of infancy for the students. If we want to preserve what we believe to be the unique contribution of P4C to education, that is, the experience of infancy, we, as teachers, need to lose our Voices, suspend the sacrament of language, and abandon the oath and the curse as modes of discoursing with students. We also cannot simply project the Voice outward (into the novel or the community of inquiry itself, both of which are proposed by Lipman). Once the Voice (in whatever form) is neutralized and the demand released from the oath, the students can finally speak and hear the event of their speech taking place. They are thrown back upon themselves (abandoned, as it were), without a frame of reference that would permit them to compare or evaluate their individual contributions in relation to some higher authority. (This also means that the students understand that whatever is being said, however factually wrong, illogical, or contradictory it may be, is not sanctioned by the facilitator.)

But what kind of speech does the teacher offer the community when his/her Voice is de-activated? What happens after the demand is exposed and has opened up a space for speaking to take place? On our account, the facilitator does not simply disappear. Indeed, the demand is faint and easily lost on the members of the community. The facilitator must *continue to hold a space for the demand* even after the space is opened. This is a risky position as one must assert the taking place of language without recourse to truth or falsehood, without the guarantee of an oath to the laws of reasonableness to point the way toward desirable outcomes. But if this is a risky position, it is also somewhat comical as the teacher-as-not-a-teacher continually undermines their Voice by asserting the positivity of language in its infancy. Here we would like to argue that speech of the teacher-as-not-a-teacher takes on the performative characteristics of the clown. The clown is a paradoxical figure who remains close to the laws of the schoolhouse, and, at the same time, abdicates all authority when it comes to the sacredness of language (what and how to speak). The clown is, simply put, the one who cannot not speak despite a lack of content or procedural knowledge. They do not take oaths or utter blasphemy (as they would certainly be killed or excommunicated). Instead, their speech is infantile, without guilt and blame, without curse or blessing. "Repeat after me, I do not know how to talk but I cannot not speak!" is itself a special kind of parody that enacts the taking and making of an oath while also profaning it in the very same gesture. But what does such speech look like in practice?

The first form is the question. On this point, we agree with P4C theorists and practitioners such as Lipman and Sharp, yet with a difference. In traditional P4C the question has a function, as defined by the ultimate criterion of reasonableness. The teacher's questions manifest an oath to this criterion and work to maintain the directionality of the speech of the students. These questions are ultimately blessed by the laws of reasonableness that they uphold. And in turn, by answering them, the students likewise make an oath (also cursing themselves). Like P4C, Agamben seems to favor the question as a privileged mode of philosophical dialogue. Indeed, several of his book titles are questions (*What Is an Apparatus?* and *What Is Philosophy?*). Yet these questions have *no function*. They do not manifest an oath to reasonableness. Instead, these questions only have a use. Use, for Agamben, is "completely emancipated from every relation to a predetermined end, in order to affirm itself."[35] Use precedes and exceeds any given function. Such questions do not know in advance where the inquiry *ought* to lead or even how it will be pursued (according to certain laws of reasonableness or democratic processes of deliberation). It rather opens up speaking to the possibility of contemplating its own infancy, its own potentiality to be spoken (which is also its impotentiality to not *not* be spoken). It is a pure affirmation of speaking that does not separate truth and lie at the onset through certain, unquestioned criteria (such as reasonableness) that determine which questions are appropriate and when it is appropriate to ask them. Instead, it is a true adventure in speaking made possible by the suspension of the sacrament of language.

The second form of speech offered by the facilitator is the parable. They do not curse or praise, as these are forms of speech that promote learning: cursing indicates what went wrong and praising indicates what went right. Yet parables teach *nothing*. They are radically inoperative forms of speech. As Franz Kafka argues, "Many complain that the words of the wise are always merely parables and of no use in daily life,"[36] hence the need for Jesus to tell the apostles the parable of the sower: because his previous parables were pedagogical "failures." The lesson of the parable seems to be silenced, and as such, educationally suspect. Yet Agamben finds in the parable a redemption of speech itself. In a biblical context, parables build similarities between this reality and the Kingdom. The Kingdom is therefore put in close proximity to what is at hand in our everyday world. The mystery and ineffability of the Kingdom become present to us through the parable, which simultaneously works to sanctify the everyday and to profane the sacred. They are, in this sense, paradoxical formulations that separate and conjoin opposites without sacrifice. Just as Jesus's parables make the beyond of the Kingdom present in this life, the parable enables us to speak that which is beyond language (language's speakability) without negation. Summarizing, Agamben writes,

> The parable on the "word of the Kingdom" is then a parable on language, that is, on what still and always remains for us to understand—our being speakers. Comprehending our dwelling in language does not mean knowing the sense of words, with all its ambiguities and subtleties. It rather means noticing that what is at stake in language is the proximity of the Kingdom, its similarity to the world—the Kingdom is so close and so similar that we struggle to acknowledge it.[37]

On our reading, the Kingdom is language's infancy, which is so close that it is easily sacrificed by language in the name of communicating this or that sense. Whereas Lipman's articulation of P4C emphasizes philosophical growth, progress, and development through the questioning of the ambiguities and subtleties of words—or in Lipman's formulation, "help children make better use of more familiar words"[38]—it is precisely the ambiguities and subtleties of parables that are to be preserved by the facilitator without Voice that ensures children have a philosophical experience of infancy. The parable thus leaves only questions that are not directed toward a destiny (learning reasonability). Instead they abandon the participants to infancy itself.

Both questions and parables expose the demand to speak (without the support of the Voice as an ultimate arbiter of truth or falseness). They are modes of speech that are infantile and thus embody, *at the same time*, both the potentiality of the lie and the truth *before* such distinctions are instituted in the form of laws of reason. They are also speech without authority that nevertheless does not abandon the position of the teacher (teacher-as-not-a-teacher, teacher as clown). Furthermore, for Lipman and Sharp, the teacher's questions are motivated by the need to help children *learn* certain dispositions oriented toward certain predetermined outcomes. The questions fulfill the oath to reasonableness. Yet in asking infantile questions and offering up parables, facilitator's speaking is not motivated by reasonable *ends*. Such speaking has no ends in sight beyond the experience of the demand to speak speaking's speakability with others. Thus what is "discovered" through P4I is not the ability to achieve an end (a destiny) so much as the forgotten means (infancy) that open language up to free use.

To conclude, we can once again return to the experience above concerning the image *Ceci n'est pas une Pipe*. In this dialogue, Tyson embodied the paradoxical location of the teacher-as-not-a-teacher. He embodied the laws of the schoolhouse by calling the class to session and by putting the image on the screen. At the same time, he rendered inoperative the authority of his own Voice by gesturing away from himself toward the image and *its* demand. Throughout the ensuing dialogue, he did not insert questions to keep students on track to learn specific dispositions in reasonabilty. Instead, his questions were prompts for the students to continue to use their own linguistic infancy to keep listening to the demand (even despite a lack of personal or shared interest). Thus, he was abnegating the professional role of the P4C facilitator whose mission it is to baptize certain kinds of speech as legitimate (as reasonable and democratic) and to model such speech through their questions. Instead, he was clowning with the students, offering strange paradoxes ("what if an actor held a pipe and pretended to smoke it, would that be a pipe or something else?" or "if an animated cartoon smoked a pipe would the drawing be a pipe because if was fulfilling its function as a pipe for the animated character?") that were themselves responses to the dialogue of the community. Like the court jester, he was in service to the use of the community but only insofar as he remained *irresponsible* toward the sacrament of language.

The Profanity of Infancy

The community of infancy is neither a sacred baptism nor merely a meaningless and empty blasphemy (of communicative capitalism). Instead of rejecting the current state of suspension by a return to the sacredness of the oath, the community of infancy offers a paradoxically profane alternative. If we are living in the eclipse of the sacrament of language, then a community of infancy offers a suspension of this suspension through an experience that no longer functions within the dialectic of the blessing and curse, of truth and falsity, of pledging and perjury. As an alternative to either the sacred Voice of the teacher (as the one who knows and thus is granted the authority to baptize) or the empty, nihilistic speech of the teacher as merely a jaded bureaucrat, what we have here is the speech of the teacher-as-not-a-teacher or as a hollow in language that keeps open the possibility for engaging in a communal experience of language's unspeakable speakability demanding to be spoken. Rather than a paradigm for the sacred function of speech, in the community of infancy language is now freed from its sacred function (based on the sacrament of language) and made available for the students to be used in new and different ways, allowing for a profane form of educational life.

This also means that educational philosophy—as an ontological inquiry into education—is always already a parody of philosophy. While philosophy attempts to reinstate the sacrament of language (and thus divide truth from falsehood, or at least provide certain analytic and empirical laws to follow on the quest), educational philosophy as a parody of this process gives philosophy an education in its own potentiality to be otherwise than the gatekeeper of truth. What we find in the philosophical practice of community of infancy is a minor practice or weak practice that does not speak the truth but rather explores what is possible when the demand (the need/necessity) of infancy carries practitioners away. On this view, the community of infancy is precisely the hinge through which education can become philosophical and philosophy can become educated. The rest of this book is one such experiment.

2

Rules

Introduction

Current approaches to doing philosophy with children range from being directed at the development of specific competences, such as the original P4C approach, to ones that are less goal-oriented but still dialogical in nature,[1] to those that use activities and are not primarily focused on dialogue.[2] While the more goal-oriented approaches have been criticized as instrumental and antithetical to the very nature of philosophy (see Introduction), approaches that are not primarily dialogical and/or lack a specific procedural framework risk being no longer recognizable as philosophical—even in a very broad sense of the term. Rather than proposing a radically new practice, we seek to demonstrate how the original P4C approach can be repotentialized by conceiving the nature and function of rules in the community of inquiry, and by extension, the community of infancy. Using Agamben's distinction between laws and rules, we argue that the rule is a unique form of educational life that produces educational freedom within a community of infancy by freeing up language for common use, while at the same time preserving the basic structure that distinguishes P4C as a specifically philosophical practice. At stake here is affirming the importance of rules while also recognizing the uniqueness of how rules constitute a community through the use of itself (as it responds to a demand).

The Question of Rules in P4C

In traditional versions of P4C the role of the teacher is defined as follows: "It is the teacher's responsibility to assure that proper procedures are being followed. But with respect to the give-and-take of philosophical discussion, the teacher must be open to the variety of views implicit among the students."[3] "Ensuring proper procedures" means that teachers regulate the dynamics of the community of inquiry without regulating the particular content (this or that philosophical position) of the dialogue that unfolds. This is meant to avoid questions of indoctrination. The P4C facilitator is only interested in *how* students think rather than *what* they think about. One way to maintain proper procedures is through the establishment of certain rules that will ensure philosophical dialogue takes place in the community and that children are encouraged to be reasonable in their thinking and ethical toward one another. As such, rules are a fundamental feature of the P4C community of inquiry (in its many shapes and sizes). For instance, Mario Biggeri and Marina Santi argue that there are basic macro-pragmatic rules that structure the kind of discourse students ought to have in a community of inquiry.[4] These rules include the following: encouraging participants to put forward their own views, reflecting before speaking, sharing relevant information, being motivated by reasoning, giving importance to thinking, accepting challenges, building on others' ideas, discussing alternatives, embracing self-correction, mediating differences, and taking on responsibility to participate in decision-making. Thomas Jackson likewise highlights certain philosophical rules of engagement that he refers to as "pillars" of P4C.[5] The rules of inquiry are spelled out by Jackson in terms of questions that facilitate the cultivation of a philosophical sensitivity. These questions include "what do you mean by," "can you give a reason for," "what are your assumptions," "what are the implications of what you are saying," "can you give an example," "are there counter examples that can be made." In addition, meta-reflection is composed of criteria that the teacher presents to the group prior to beginning the inquiry and again at the end of the process. Jackson gives two sets of criteria: those focused on the dynamics of the community (was listening practiced, for instance) and the inquiry itself (did it maintain focus, stimulate interest, and so forth). In short, the rules that form the pillars of P4C include certain questions that maintain an emphasis on critical thinking and criteria that evaluate the quality of the dialogue as a whole. Finally, David Kennedy discusses rules in the context of community of inquiry practice as a particular speech situation. For young children, most learning concerns the internalization of implicit rules such as when and how to speak, what discursive patterns are acceptable, and which vocabularies are valued. Kennedy also emphasizes how there are "no fixed rules for what can or cannot be part of community of inquiry curriculum."[6] Instead, the rules apply to the way the community operates.

As Lipman makes clear, such rules need not be spelled out and memorized by the participants in a community of inquiry. He states, "It would be well to mention here that, in teaching thinking skills, one does not necessarily begin by teaching rules, axioms, and definitions from which the remainder of the subject is to be inferred by rigorous deduction."[7] Instead, when it comes to children, a more "holistic approach" should be adopted where rules are learned through the dialogue itself. This avoids problems of mechanistic application. Through the proper procedure (as facilitated by the teacher), children can become intuitively sensitive to the "look and feel of illogic"[8] and subtly "habituated" into asking questions at the right time in the right way. And then, when a certain growth, development, or progress is achieved, Lipman concedes that the rules (already internalized) can be made explicit. Or, as in his original model, rules can be spelled out as needed through didactic teaching that momentarily interrupts the dialogue and reminds participants about proper dynamics.

As one can see, which rules are appropriate and how these rules are introduced to children to promote a philosophical disposition are key features of the proper procedure of P4C. We do not take issue with this, but we do want to highlight how emphasis is often placed on what the rules should be (hence Lipman's exhaustive lists of criteria, fallacies, dispositions, and skills) and how they should be employed rather than on what a rule *is*. This is interesting as one of the P4C children's novels, *Lisa*, explicitly raises the question of rules in relation to standards. Yet when it comes to a social-ontological investigation into the status of the rule in its own practice, P4C has not been so self-reflexive. In other words, there is no philosophy of the rule in P4C. Rules, in this sense, are taken for granted as unproblematic infrastructure supporting the community's inquiry. They are, to use phenomenological language, so close and familiar to the practice that they almost disappear into the background. It is instructive that the ontology of rules is absent from the key questions highlighted in the recent handbook of philosophy for children (nor is "rule" listed in this book's index).[9] Yet it is our contention that rules as such (not this or that particular rule) should be pulled out of this implicit background and placed squarely in the foreground of the practice. To do so is to pose some questions to rules and how they are used in the community, including "[w]hat is a rule and how does it differ from a law?" Such a question demands philosophical reflection on the nature and function of rules in relation to communities of practice. By clarifying the idea of a rule, we hope to further open up a space for P4I within the P4C literature, as P4I pushes the logic of rules to the limit point where rules dissolve into the community (and the community into its own rules), whose ultimate form of speaking is nothing other than speaking speaking's speakability.

Monastic Rules versus Laws

To help clarify the status of rules, we will use Agamben's discussion of the nature of rules in monastic communities (and the Franciscan monastic order, in particular) in his book *The Highest Poverty: Monastic Rules and Form-of-Life*. This turn to the monastery might seem paradoxical given the critique of education-as-sacred in contemporary educational philosophy. As argued in the last chapter, educational theorists Ivan Illich and Jan Masschelein and Maarten Simons, for example, have described institutionalized schooling as a modernized, secular church, full of rituals, sacraments, and various incantations, with the teacher acting as a "priest" looking out for the flock. The reason Agamben's depiction of monastic communities can be used in a positive/constructive way is that he sees monasticism as a form of (religious) life that is itself opposed to the institution of the church. Indeed, we might go so far as to say that for Agamben, Franciscan monasticism is a kind of *profanation* of the very idea of the sacred endorsed by the church.

What makes it so, for Agamben, is that the rules that organize monastic life are not fashioned after and do not function as laws—not only the laws of the church, but laws, or the law, in general. When Agamben uses the term "law" he means "the entire text of tradition in its regulative form."[10] In other words, law refers to explicit and implicit forms of regulation that condition the lived facticity of human experience in the world. There are two dimensions to this regulation: force and signification. Force ensures that there are pressures to follow the law (these pressures might be wide as in implicit social pressures or narrow in the sense of pressures exerted by explicit, juridical laws). The law is administered from above, or from outside the community. It is therefore transcendent of the community itself, standing in judgment over the community. Such judgment might be in the name of the community or for the community's best interests, but it is not, in itself, immanent to the community—hence the need for force to ensure that the community measures up to the measure of the law. Signification means that there is content to be followed (prescriptions for normative behavior). We might think of this as the model of the law as operative in its average, everyday level. Law regulates from above (providing content to actions) and ensures that actions abide by law through threat of force.

But for Agamben, there is a legitimation crisis with the law that has become the norm within the contemporary moment. Here the law remains in force but without content. Drawing on Kafka's parable "Before the Law," Agamben highlights the paradoxical force of the law to regulate life precisely in the moment of its radical emptiness. In other words, law becomes supremely powerful when it regulates nothing and prescribes nothing. Summarizing Kafka's insight, Agamben argues that "law is all the more pervasive for its total lack of content."[11] This is the "summit and root of every law."[12] The key to Agamben's analysis of the paradox of the law is that the law is at its maximal power at the precise moment in which it applies to life by not applying, when its force is *pure*, meaning formal and empty. In such instances, anything appears possible—any gesture can be turned into the occasion for a trial. This, for Agamben, marks the distinctive features of modern totalitarian states. Within a state of emergency, law and life become "indistinguishable"[13] precisely because law is nothing more than an empty force. When the force of law merges with life, the result is abandonment of life to force, or what Agamben refers to as bare life. Agamben summarizes: "[I]nsofar as law is maintained as pure form in a state of virtual exception, it lets bare life … subsist before it."[14] Bare life is life abandoned to the force of the law and as such can be killed with impunity. Bare life is therefore subject directly to the sovereign who decides whose life is worth living.

Against this backdrop it is interesting to compare Agamben's notion of rules. For instance, Agamben claims, "The rule, whose model is the Gospel, cannot therefore have the form of law, and it is probable that the very choice of the term *regula* implied an opposition to the sphere of the legal."[15] Indeed, the rule is "radically heterogeneous to institutions and law" and is an attempt to "realize a human life and practice absolutely outside the determinations of the law."[16] Stated simply the difference is as follows: the law becomes indistinguishable from life insofar as it is contentless whereas rules become indistinguishable from life insofar as they merge with it through infinite self-generation and self-constitution. Laws and rules converge and diverge in the zone of indistinguishability from life, but one is from above (a sovereign decision) and the other is from below (from within the community). Rules, as exemplified in the monastic tradition, are a formulization of the implicit, preexisting practices in a community. They are, simply put, expositions of the form-of-life within a community by a community. They give form to the life *as it is being lived* within the community, and what is lived, gives life to this form. As Agamben states, "The rule is not applied to life, but produces it and at the same time is produced in it."[17] The two are, in other words, indistinguishable, hence the entanglement of form and life in the formula form-of-life. The application of the law results in bare life separated from its form, whereas the entanglement and indistinguishability of rule and life result in a form-of-life without separation. We might think of rules as *content without force*. In other words, there is no commandment to follow; there is no authority of the sovereign to proclaim a state of exception; there is no superior principle to strive to embody. Rules are not requirements that can be judged against a life but are the form-of-life that has taken a vow. While the vow itself might be contentless, the key here is that the vow opens a space for a life to emerge with its own specific content. As Agamben writes, rules are not norms to be applied to a community from the outside. In other words, "there is no place for anything like an application of the law to life"[18] when one is operating within the terrain of rules. The rule neutralizes the relationship between norm and action (which results in a sovereign judgment) opting instead for the immanence of rule with life. In fact, we could argue that rules are only possible through the *deposing* of laws in the act of living a life that forms its own rule. Finally, unlike the law that, in the state of exception, appears as a necessary fact of the sovereign's will, rules are contingent upon the life of the community. This contingency means that rules concern new uses that can emerge when laws are neutralized. In sum, Agamben argues that when rules and life enter into a zone of indifference, "they allow a third thing to appear, which the Franciscans, albeit without succeeding in defining it with precision will call 'use.'"[19] Use, in this context, refers to that which does not have a predefined function, identity, or destiny. When rule and life enter into the threshold of indifference, the possibility for *free* use is introduced into the world.

> In short, we can summarize as follows:
> Operative laws = force + content
> Inoperative laws = force – content
> Rules = content – force

Rules are a form-of-life in that they are formed within life and sustained within the life of a community without reliance on any transcendental force to ensure their operativity. They are, in this sense, purely immanent to life. The *forceless content* of the rule gives back form to life whereas the contentless force of inoperative laws takes form away from life by separating it into bare life.

The unique relationship to rules constitutes the nature of monastic communities: (1) monastic life is intrinsically communal; (2) there is a complete merging of the life of monks and their religious practice; and (3) the community is based on the maxim of poverty. The latter is especially important for the way in which rules function in the monastic community because renouncing the right to own things (individually or collectively) undermines one of the most prominent tenets and applications of the law (ownership, property)—which by itself places the community outside the law (judicial realm). Instead of ownership *over* a community (predetermining who is included and excluded or what counts as legitimate and illegitimate participation), rules concern use of a community by itself in the act of its self-generation.

Functionality of Rules and Laws in P4C

Perhaps the problem with the traditional P4C approach is a confusion between rules and laws. We need to make a critical distinction that draws on and further develops ideas from the last chapter. It is important to return to Lipman's quote above about when to reveal the rules that children have already been taught (on an intuitive level) through dialogue. Notice that the "rules" *precede* the community and come from the outside. They are imported by the teacher who ensures a proper procedure. If the rules emerged from within the community itself, then Lipman's problem of mechanical application would not arise. Mechanical application of rules only becomes a problem when the rules are somehow beyond the community, and the community must approximate these rules. Even if rules are habituated over time through the practice itself, this does not mean that the question of the *origin* of the rules is solved. Instead, the origin is merely concealed from the children. Furthermore, Lipman emphasizes the habituation of rules so they become second nature. Sharp makes a similar claim, arguing that "in time"[20] children who practice P4C internalize the process of giving and expecting reasons, respecting persons as individuals, subjecting ideas to critical inquiry, etc. These rules are never questioned, they are merely internalized and then later revealed as rules (but only after they have become an indisputable feature of the identity of the community). In short, the inside of the community comes to it from the outside.

Bearing this in mind, we want to propose that *there are no rules* in traditional P4C, only laws. In P4C, there is sometimes an attempt to draw distinctions between laws and rules. For instance, Kennedy discusses procedural and speech rules that regulate the behaviors of the community of inquiry as distinct from the laws of formal and informal logic that act as the ultimate "referee" in dialogue.[21] Yet the distinction begins to break down when we recognize that what counts as a viable procedural or speech "rule" is predicated on maintaining the laws of formal and informal logic as the ultimate referee. In this sense, the rules emerge not from the community but from the inner workings of logic itself. Or perhaps more forcefully, these laws command identification of the community with the law through the rules *it* institutes. Lipman writes, dialogue counts as dialogue only when it is "disciplined by logic."[22] If the dialogue begins to waver from this discipline under the tutelage of logic, the Voice of the teacher can intervene in the dialogue to maintain compliance and ensure that the law is fulfilled. Another way of saying this would be that the Voice of the teacher intervenes when the disciplinary *force* of the law of logic is threatened, as evidenced through the transgression of the law's rule. This interrelationship between law and Voice is most manifest in a moment when the function of both is in jeopardy. Case in point: Lipman's diary entry from April 1, 1982, which was written after he facilitated a dialogue about his book *Pixie* with fourth graders. Lipman writes, "Sometimes a discussion will take off in an unexpected direction and go so well that you forget to follow up some of the more obvious leads, with the result that the discussion, for all its exhilarating quality, lacks the proper cognitive closure."[23] The facilitator is there to ensure that the dialogue moves toward a rendezvous with its destiny (reasonableness) according to the discipline of logic. The dialogue thus is a means to achieving a definitive end that is safeguarded by the facilitator who is there to maintain a course. The P4C facilitator uses certain kinds of functional questions and makes certain kinds of interventions in order to guarantee that the laws of logic are actualized and verified in the speech of the children. Lipman's lament recorded in the diary indicates a sense of failure. Why? Because he did not successfully embody the Voice of the teacher and as a consequence, the exchange might have been exhilarating, but it did not achieve the stature of a dialogue. Things were interesting but the proper lesson was not learned. The disciplinary force of the law of logic failed, producing aberrant speech that did not culminate in cognitive closure.

While the Voice of the facilitator might be needed to create the conditions necessary for the development of certain kinds of learners (reasonable subjects prepared for democratic citizenship, for instance), it sacrifices what is essentially philosophical about the community: the experience of infancy. To open up the possibility for the community to experiment with language—and thus experiment with philosophy in relation to a demand—we need to maintain the possibility for the community to define itself in relation to is capacity for speech (rather than to laws of logic that must discipline it). The question is how we can reconceive the way rules function in P4I, in order to reduce the juridical nature and lawful execution of the practice, while, at the same time, preserving the procedural framework that makes such experimentation possible in the first place.

Returning to Agamben's discussion of the nature of monastic rules, we can say that what would change the juridical nature of the community of inquiry is, first of all, to think of the community as sufficient (in terms of what it already is), namely a group of human beings that can speak, rather than needing speech to become something else. Having the community see itself as such corresponds to the monks' pledge of poverty—only that here it is a pledge of intellectual poverty: renouncing the need to know or acquire specific skills or abilities according to a law of reasonableness. Like the monastic community, it is this first step of a renunciation of the need to own things that establishes the community from its inception as operating outside of the law of education. Another way of saying this would be that P4I opens a space and time for the participants to produce the form-of-life defining their community without recourse to a power outside of itself (the force of the law of reasonableness and the content of the rules that serve as its embodiment). Rules allow the community to be whatever it cannot not be according to a demand.

Instead of laws preceding the community and inserted from the outside, rules are generated as a form-of-life that produces itself. Rules *proceed* (rather than precede) from the community. The rules are not what are to be internalized so much as what are to be formulated from the practice as it emerges and comes in contact with its own infantile potentiality (see Chapter 3). And indeed, anyone who has practiced some form of philosophical community of inquiry with children will experience the excitement of children reflecting on and continually modifying the rules of their own practice. For instance, to use an example from our own experience, students in one of our P4I sessions invented the following rule: when responding, one must raise a hand and indicate with fingers how many times one has already contributed to the dialogue. In another case, a group of students engaged in P4C through an online Zoom interface invented the rule that one can use the chat function to make meta-comments about the dialogue. This self-constitution of the community out of itself is what is *most philosophical* in the community dynamic, returning the community to its own potentiality or infancy as inseparable from the form-of-life that it takes up.

In this way, Agamben enables us to give further clarity to the quality of the "emergent structure" of the communal rules highlighted by Nadia Kennedy and David Kennedy.[24] Insightfully, Kennedy and Kennedy argue that the laws of logic Lipman attempted to import into the community through subtle, prolonged exposure to guided dialogue are—more or less—to be found in the everyday rules of speech within communities. These include making distinctions and comparisons, clarifying concepts, generating analogies, combining propositions into syllogisms, and so forth. What is important here is that the rules are *internal* and *constituent* of the everyday language of the participants. They are not added to the language as a disciplining force from the outside. They are, in this sense, always already the implicit form of speaking that children adopt without any supplemental force being added. We agree with Kennedy and Kennedy that respect for the sufficiency of the community and its way of speaking is essential for sidestepping the problem of disciplinary force that one encounters with Lipman's model (and by extension, the function of the Voice of the teacher). On our reading, P4I uniquely turns attention toward these intrinsic rules as the conditions for community. Through P4I, these existing rules can themselves be spoken and thought about—not as means to another end (the promotion of a certain kind of speaking) but as pure means or pure use of the community by itself to fashion itself (thus open to revision or addition through studious play, see Chapter 3). P4I allows children to experience rules structuring their interactions as rules—as the form that their living is taking in its enactment. These are not rules that are learned. Rather, students are *exposed* to the rules of language as they are named in the course of speaking with one another.

But there are two problems here. For Kennedy and Kennedy, the rules that matter in the everyday speech of children seem to still be predicated on the laws of reasonableness (certain normative assumptions about the proper way to speak within ideal speech situations). Their list only includes rules that, in the last instance, are "legitimate" in relation to laws that transcend (and bless) them. These are the rules that matter, and they matter because logic says so! Our claim is more radical in that the rules are *whatever* they are. They need not appeal to stronger laws outside of themselves to be recognized as legitimate. Instead, the work of legitimizing rules ought to remain the focus of the community itself as it is exposed to its own rules-in-the-naming. Second, Kennedy and Kennedy seem to stop at these rules as *ends in themselves*. In other words, the goal is to reveal the rules, how they work, and in turn, how they can be used more effectively and efficiently in learning how to be reasonable, deliberative subjects. Yet for us, rules are how a community *freely uses itself* in relation to a demand (rather than in relation to a law). Or, stated differently, rules are how a demand structures itself into a form-of-life that is livable.

In using itself to form itself (through its rules), the community of infancy encounters the demand of its own infancy and through this demand, has an opportunity to contemplate its potentiality. Contemplation is not a more conscious and deliberative deployment of everyday speech rules (in order to become more reasonable or solve a problem) so much as the exposure of the potentiality experienced in the emergence of a form-of-life. Agamben writes, "[C]ontemplation does not have an object, because in the work it contemplates only its (own) potential."[25] Contemplation is a putting aside content and force and instead turns toward potentiality, infancy as such. Agamben continues, "[I]n contemplation, the work is deactivated and rendered inoperative, and in this way, restored to possibility, opened to a new possible use."[26] Contemplation returns the community to that which is most basic and that which is most taken for granted: the speakability of language in its infancy (without force or content). Speakability (*that* there is language to be spoken) makes an appearance not *as* the rules (and how they ought to be employed) but rather *through* the naming of rules (and how this ultimately hits upon their ground in speakability).

Think of moments when the community of philosophers turns to itself and asks of itself "*how* are we"? In such instances, the infancy experienced in taking up and employing rules of self-formation shows itself, not as content or as force but as a question of what needs to be in place for the community to be whatever it is. This is a moment of contemplating the community's potentiality to be a community. In P4I, this experience of contemplation is commonized. In so doing, P4I makes contemplation free in ways that Agamben does not fully take into account. Indeed, Agamben's major figures of contemplation remain largely isolated and singular rather than communal. In communal contemplation such as P4I, there is no cognitive closure (as ensured by the Voice of the teacher). Instead, what we find is linguistic *disclosure*, or language revealing its own potentiality, which is infantile and undestined. Contemplating the infantile nature of rules creates the condition for a community that is not negative or destined so much as full of potentiality. Contemplation on this view is not a time for "gathering thoughts" but for contemplating speakability, for sensing the collective potentiality to speak without thereby saying anything except sayability itself. Participants suddenly ask, "What is it that lets you say that?" (not in relation to laws of reasonableness but in terms of the ontology of infancy and its demand). These kinds of questions are contemplative in nature, meaning that they are a thinking of speech's speakability or communication's communicability.

Rules ensure that the community is irreparable, meaning that it is not attempting to become something other than whatever it is. For Agamben, the irreparable is "that things are just as they are, in this or that mode, consigned without remedy to their way of being."[27] The community is not striving to reach a goal beyond itself (and thus live up to the expectations of a law), but rather to experiment with its own self formation through its rules. It is important to note that such sufficiency (the community of P4I is whatever it is) is not merely an acceptance of existing qualities nor is an attempt to produce new qualities to replace the old ones. It is rather a way of *reexperiencing* old qualities (such as its implicit rules of speaking) as full of potentiality. If traditional P4C practice needs laws (instead of rules), it is because the force of the law is what intervenes and keeps the content of the speech of the community on the right track toward a specific, predefined goal: reasonableness. We might even argue that such laws are the way in which the sanctity of speech introduced in the last chapter is operationalized, or made into a form of governmentality over speech. Yet in P4I, the core experience is not one of growth, development, or progress toward an actualization of this law in the form of increasingly reasonable speech. The core experience is rather the quality of having the capability to speak (as a potentiality) emerging from the contemplation of rules (how a community is whatever it is). Agamben summarizes, "Assuming my being-such, my manner of being, is not assuming this or that quality, this or that character, virtue or vice, wealth or poverty. My qualities and my being-thus are not qualifications of a substance (of a subject) that remains behind them and that I would truly be. I am never *this* or *that*, but always *such*, *thus*."[28] To be such and thus is therefore not to claim a particular identity as a possession ("I am reasonable") or as a goal to be obtained ("I am developing reasoning skills"), but rather to experience one's potentiality to speak within the speech one has. Being-thus is the exposure of the potentiality to speak (and not to speak) within speech and thus maintains that speech is always open for free use. Indeed it is this free use that is *demanded* by infancy.

Finally, it should be noted that what is being shared and held in common (not owned or possessed, only used) in this kind of community is language. Common use of language means not speaking in a particular, predetermined way, not claiming ownership over language. It is this experience of the necessity of language to be contingent that Agamben calls infancy, and it is precisely this communal experience of infancy—made possible in a community based on rules rather than laws—that repotentializes (revitalizes) the community of inquiry as a community of infancy. Rules are an essential feature of the community of inquiry (qua community of infancy), precisely because they are the manifestation of the love of the community for its freedom to define its own form of educational life (through a common use of language).

The Facilitator and Rule Formation

Of course, the space and time for this experience is carved out by the facilitator who allows a demand to manifest itself/be exposed. This intervention is not arbitrary, but rather absolutely necessary given the context of the school, wherein a rupture must happen with the classroom norms. In other words, uttering an inoperative, parodic (comedic?) oath that silences the silence of the Voice of the teacher is needed to carve out a space and time that is noninstrumental against a highly instrumental, standardized background. As such, P4I recognizes the importance of the facilitator's gesture of suspending the operativity of the laws of learning and thereby create a space and time for the use of speech as a response to the demand of infancy.

The paradox here is interesting to note, especially in relation to Agamben's analysis of sovereignty in the political realm outlined above. For Agamben, the sovereign is the one who has the power to suspend the operativity of the law, creating a state of exception from above. In this exceptional state, life is stripped bare of its content, leaving only nude life (*zoe*). As such, the law is in force without content in a state of totalitarian excess. Connecting Agamben's notion of sovereignty with that of the Voice introduced in Chapter 1, we can argue that the sovereign creates bare life precisely because of the negativity of the Voice itself (which is always predicated on some kind of mysterious, powerful, extra-linguistic and extra-juridical power that remains unsayable). The sovereign is the one whose Voice suspends the law in order to save the law (and in the process, produces the exceptional state through which life is put at risk of abandonment). As an alternative, Agamben gestures toward Walter Benjamin's notion of the state of exception *from below*, which he describes as a real state of exception that is inaugurated by the oppressed in opposition to their oppressors. Here the state of exception does not concern domination and exploitation so much as liberation via revolutionary action as workers (for instance) leave the factory and flood into the streets to protest. Whereas the sovereign makes a decision based on the Voice (and its negativity), the masses respond to an internal demand (a necessity to constitute itself out of its own practices) and in doing so manifest the potentiality that is always already present yet not destined for this or that kind of work within the given order. One is negative (resulting in sacrifice or abandonment) and the other purely affirmative (resulting in revolution against oppression). As such, Agamben and his Benjaminian inheritances suggest that there are two kinds of exceptional states (above and below) that have very different political effects.

In the classroom, the facilitator of P4I also suspends a special law: the law of learning. This law ensures that educational outcomes can be identified in relation to growth, development, and progress and measured in relation to certain predefined outcomes. The teacher thus curses the law of learning that defines the schoolhouse. But unlike the sovereign power described by Agamben, here the suspension opens up a space where the rules defining the content for a philosophical form-of-educational-life can emerge. This state of emergency from above provides the conditions for a break with learning pressures and regulations over life so that life can live its own livability through philosophical inquiry. This is not a state of exception called forth from below, which would place the burden on children and young adults to force a neutralization of learning's powers of control. Instead, the adult takes up this responsibility and uses his or her "sovereignty" to transform the speaking conditions in the classroom. Or perhaps better phrased, the adult teacher-as-not-a-teacher takes up this irresponsibility and uses sovereignty in a parodic, profane, comical way to open up a space and time for speaking that is not beholden to the kinds of speaking determined in advance as acceptable, reasonable, and democratic according to the law of learning. As such, P4I offers a paradoxical formulation not found in Agamben's work that can be schematized as follows:

1. The law is enforced (everyday law)
    a. Social level: enforcement of legal duties and responsibilities as citizens
    b. Educational level: enforcement of the law of learning through scheduled testing and evaluation
2. The enforcement of law is suspended by a sovereign decision (state of exception from above)
    a. Social level: production of bare life (without content) as a life that can be sacrificed, excluded from a community
    b. Educational level: abandonment of students as educational subjects through various forms of suspension[29]
3. The enforcement of the law is suspended by the subaltern or the workers (state of exception from below)
    a. Social level: political revolution
    b. Educational level: student protests
4. The enforcement of the law of learning is suspended by a profane decision to expose the demand (a state of exception from above that nevertheless potentializes life from below)
    a. Educational level (exclusively): community of infancy wherein the community is allowed to carve out a place where a form-of-life can rule itself within (yet against) the law of learning (dominant in the schoolhouse)

This means that "sovereignty" of the teacher in an educational setting is not identical to that we find in the political realm and can be turned into a *positive* rather than purely negative foundation for a community. But this only holds true insofar as the teacher-as-not-a-teacher embodies a weak, profane, parodic, and comical form of sovereignty (a sovereignty without force when it comes to students). What is sacrificed here is not life under a law but rather a law itself (and its force) in the classroom—as that which has been deactivated and held in abeyance—so that rules *from below* can emerge to define a collective form-of-life. Holding these laws of learning in suspension means that the teacher-as-not-a-teacher does not risk abandoning the lives of those exposed to a lawless condition so much as he or she risks his or her own status as a "responsible," "professional," and "effective" teacher whose identity is certified by the state and its expectations for professionalism. Indeed, the teacher-as-not-a-teacher is, as previously argued, a clown that always risks such labels precisely because they simultaneously must neighbor the laws of the schoolhouse while also suspending their Voice in relation to students. Thus sovereigns, in this case, actually risk abandoning themselves, turning sovereignty into a kind of bare life (that can be punished by the law of the schoolhouse that dictates productivity, efficacy, and efficiency over the classroom and its management).

Conclusion

The move from laws to rules may seem like a relatively slight or minor shift. What makes it significant is that, from an Agambenian perspective, the monastic community (and Franciscanism in particular) represents "the attempt to realize a human life and practice absolutely outside the determinations of the law," pointing to "the possibility of a human existence beyond the law."[30] In the same way, we could say that P4C, conceived as P4I, allows us to think a radically different form-of-educational-life outside of the determinations of the law of learning (and, more generally, beyond an idea of education based on laws), that is, beyond the mere acquisition and possession of knowledge, skills, dispositions, or abilities that allow for the experience of a radical openness toward possible ways of speaking, thinking, and acting that could also be seen as a prerequisite for any kind of genuine/meaningful education. Rules are therefore necessary for an educational experience in common use. But because rules are themselves immanent to the form-of-life in the community, they can be turned into a question and, for a moment, rendered inoperative through contemplation. The result, from the outside, might appear to be educationally poor or a waste of time: a community left with nothing but its rules (always provisional and emergent) and thus lacking the laws (of learning) that would guarantee significant cognitive closure (as Lipman so desired). Yet moments of contemplation are not an absence or deficit. Rather they can be read otherwise as experiences of reflecting on the very conditions of possibility underlying rule formation. What is left is nothing other than the community in potential, without negation or destiny, a community that is whatever it is.

3

Adventure

In the last chapter, we established the quality of thinking found in P4I (contemplation) in relation to rules (as the form given to the use of the community by itself through contemplation). In this chapter, we will turn our attention to focus on the quality of the speech when speech speaks its own speakability. Our inspiration for this chapter is Lipman's emphasis on the "irresistible adventure"[1] that education can be. Lipman and colleagues write,

> But why cannot the child's entire school experience be an adventure? It should be chockfull of opportunities for surprise, with the tension of exciting possibilities, with tantalizing mysteries to be wondered at as well as with fascinating clarifications and illuminations. … Adventure is satisfying in and of itself, one dwells so often in memory on one's past adventures that it is as though they somehow contained, like dreams, the secret meaning of one's life. … [A]dventure, never free of risk and delightful uncertainty, is what the child's reveries suggest life ought to be.[2]

Here, adventure is specified as "opportunities for surprise," "tension of exciting possibilities," and "mysteries." It is full of risks and uncertainty but also contains the secret meaning of one's life. Because of this last criterion, adventure appears to be the very heart of philosophical inquiry. Philosophy is not so much about cultivating skills or dispositions in critical thinking as it is defining the existential meaning of one's life. Yet it is precisely this risk and uncertainty that is what is often sacrificed when P4C takes an instrumental turn and aligns itself with the discourses and practices of the learning society (as discussed in the introduction to this book). Without adventure, philosophy turns into yet another skillset and inquiry, into yet another operationalized and thus measurable metric under the law of learning. Such approaches denude philosophy of its adventure.

To help return to and preserve the adventure of philosophy, it is our wager that we need to articulate the qualities of speech found within the community of infancy. In particular, we will focus on how infantile speech is akin to babble and how the community of infancy is a special kind of contemplation best described as *studious play* with this babble. The adventure in thinking that defines the community's practice emerges from studious play with speech, or rather, with the speakability of speech (an experiment not in what can be said so much as a demand *that* language be said in what can be said). In this sense, the real experiment that Lipman hints at is not found outside of language but is rather the act of speaking as such. Risk here is always the risk of attempting to speak not just this or that idea, concept, proposition, or belief but rather speaking speech's speakability and thus manifesting its infancy. And, in the end, this is no deep mystery (a hidden essence or telos below the surface of experience), but rather an encounter with an outside that is so close it is inside, and an inside that is so far it is outside: the communicability that pronounces itself through our trembling manners.

But before this description can get underway, it is imperative to outline the kinds of speech that normally circulate throughout a classroom. As Lipman first recognized, children's speech is often highly limited and constrained in typical classroom settings. He worries, "[I]n many classrooms talking has a bad name, and students' efforts to engage in it covertly are treated as evidence of disobedience rather than as evidence of healthy impulses needing only to be effectively organized so as to be harnessed in the service of education."[3] Reiterating this point, Sharp also worries, "Schools are often places where teachers do most of the talking and children mostly listen. If children do talk, they talk about things that teachers think they should talk about."[4] Expanding on these basic insights, we might argue that there are typically three types of legitimate speech in a classroom. First, there is speech as confirmation. This might be speech as confirmation of an assignment done or order followed ("Yes, Mr. L, I completed my homework"). Second, we might find examples of speech as an explanation of a wrongdoing ("I didn't complete the homework because my dog ate my notes!"). Finally, there is speech that illustrates learning has happened. This is perhaps the most educationally relevant form of speech found in a classroom as it testifies to a successful transaction between teacher and student ("The answer is the 5th Amendment!"). Notice, none of these forms of speech embody the act of thinking. They might confirm that thinking of some kind has taken place, but they themselves do not enact thinking. There is, in other words, a strict division between thinking and speaking. Speaking only conveys something that has already happened (that something has been completed, that something has been thought through, that something has been learned). Speech (as thinking, as inquiry) does not conform to these types and thus acquires a "bad name," as Lipman points out. It is also important to note that when speech and thinking are separated, speech can only act as a kind of oath that testifies to what has or has not happened/been learned. It can only curse or bless what a student says. In this sense, we are once again stuck in a cycle where speaking as oath-taking always already contains the kernel of blasphemy against the student within speech (see Chapter 1).

As opposed to these models, P4C opts for a different experience of thinking and speaking: one that does not separate the two acts but rather conjoins them through inquiry. Speaking, in P4C, is an act of joining back together that which has been split apart: thinking and speaking. The dialogue is therefore alive with thinking, and students discover what they think through their speaking. Dialogue, for Lipman, actively "sharpens the child's reasoning skills as nothing else can."[5] This is why dialogic practice is so important for rethinking how to do philosophy (with children or with adults). This is precisely why P4C is adventurous for Lipman: there are stakes in speaking because through speaking, one discovers one's thoughts. We agree with Lipman and P4C advocates as to the importance of speaking and its relationship to thinking. Yet there is still a problem with this model. In finding thought *through* collective speaking, *speech disappears*. And when this happens, the adventure of education that Lipman wanted to preserve is itself sacrificed. Such an adventure might not be as effectively organized or harnessed as Lipman had desired, but it nevertheless is a unique opportunity to think about infancy in and through one's speaking. In P4I, *speaking makes its appearance as that which is to be thought*. It is not a mere instrument for giving birth to the act of thinking. Rather the mediality of language to carry thought reveals itself in its infancy as what ought to be thought. And *this* is what is most adventurous precisely because it renders inoperative the laws of learning that can evaluate speech according to predetermined success conditions.

The starting point for thinking the adventure offered by P4I is actually Lipman's philosophical text *Pixie*, which, in our estimation, is the critical piece of fiction written by Lipman precisely because it foregrounds language. *Pixie* is unique in the Lipman catalog because it not only utilizes language to convey thought, but actually makes language *appear* as a concern for thought. As Sharp so eloquently puts it, *Pixie* is "a story of language inquiring about itself."[6] The character Brian attempts to understand the relationship between thinking, meaning, and himself, and in so doing, stumbles upon the speakability of language. It is our argument that Brian has undergone an adventure in the strict philosophical sense. With *Pixie* in mind, we want to liberate the adventurousness of education alluded to by Lipman, but to do so we have to suspend the dominant tendency in his thought toward harnessing this adventure, and thus denuding it of that which makes it adventurous in the first place: the appearance of infancy. It also means that the philosopher need not write philosophical novels for children so much as adventurous fables for studious play!

From Operative Inquiry to Inoperative Infancy

What kind of linguistic experiment is P4C? On the more or less traditional view, P4C is a linguistic experiment that concerns developing reasonable thinking. To do so, it promotes dialogue in a community of inquiry where the facilitator only intervenes in order to promote more thinking through certain kinds of questions. In this model, P4C accepts the existence of speech as the taken-for-granted background out of which a community of inquiry can come to define itself, its goals, and its procedures. Yet for Agamben, the real philosophical experience is first and foremost the wonder at the appearance of speech as such.

Infancy, as we have been arguing, is an experiment in language that wonders at its very appearance as language. Through such experimentation, language speaks its own (un)speakable speakability. Infancy in this sense is both *inside and outside of language simultaneously* or is a form of speaking that recursively recalls the (in)capacity for speech within speech. Infancy is poised between animal *phone* and human *logos*. It thus does not sacrifice either and instead holds them both in suspension. As such, infancy is without negation (as it affirms the zone of contact between speech and nonspeech). It is also without destiny (as it does not have a prescribed purpose, goal, or telos guiding it or measuring its progress, development, or growth). An experiment with language that does not negate and does not have a destiny opens speaking up to its own potentiality to be spoken, speakability, or communicability. This is the infancy in speech that P4C presupposes but does not theorize.

Here are several examples drawn from Agamben's work that throw into relief the experience of speakability. Commenting on the work of poet Giovanni Pascoli who was fascinated by dead languages, Agamben theorizes that "thought lives off the death of words."[7] But what is a dead word? It is a word that, when heard, sounds like a word but does not convey any specific meaning. Dead words, writes Agamben, "signify without signification."[8] Although dead, such words signify the potentiality to signify. Let loose from any determinate function or meaning, what dead words give us is the experience of language as such, of a pure language. In this strange way, the death of words and their infancy come to correspond in a state of indistinction.

We might also recall Agamben's analysis of *glossolalia* or speaking in a foreign tongue. Agamben writes, "If I utter words whose meaning I do not understand, he who speaks in me, the voice that utters them, the very principle of speech in me, will be something barbarous, something that does not know how to speak and that does not know what it says. To-speak-in-gloss is thus to experience in oneself barbarian speech, speech that one does not know; it is to experience an 'infantile' speech … in which understanding is 'unfruitful.'"[9] *Glossolalia* does not lend itself to understanding but rather to the pure experience of language as a potentiality for meaning, a pure potentiality for translation without being translated.

While Agamben finds these experiments with language important and interesting, they are also limited. As articulated in the introduction of this book, language (in Western philosophy) is founded on negation. Dead languages can only experience the potentiality of language through death, and speaking in a foreign tongue can only happen through the assumption of barbarism. In poetry, we can experience the appearance of language as a pure means, but to do so is, for Agamben, to experience the letter of poetry as a "place of death."[10] This is a major problem as it founds infancy on negation rather than affirmation. As such, Agamben poses the question: "Can there be speech, poetry, and thought beyond the letter, beyond the death of the voice and the death of language?"[11] This would be an experiment with language that takes up the infancy found in dead languages and *glossolalia* but does not replicate yet another form of death.

One such experience might be found in Agamben's theory of babbling. For Agamben, babbling is a unique linguistic experiment in the pure appearance of language that does not appear to be predicated on a negation or on death. Instead, it is predicated on natality and birth. The "babble of infancy"[12] should not be taken strictly as biological or developmental in nature as a state out of which the "adult" emerges equipped with a grammar that ensures communication. Indeed, the babble of infancy is always with us in those moments when we are seized upon by the happening of language (its very speakability) as it interrupts and suspends the smooth communication of any given content or message. Connecting babble back with our previous discussion of rules in Chapter 2 we can offer the following definition of babble: speech that speaks its own rules of possibility, therefore repotentializing itself for new use. And in so speaking these rules (making its own potentiality its content), babble exposes us to the infantile potentiality of language. Babble is not reducible to the rules but rather is the speech that speaks the rules of its own speakability, or the speech that interrupts and suspends its communicative function by exposing its origins. Exposure opens up language to an experiment through use (an adventure, as we will see below). And in this sense, babble is beyond (or perhaps before) cursing and blessing, which always split language from itself (or thinking from speaking and speaking from thinking).

This emphasis on babbling also connects with Agamben's notes on jargon. In much of political theory, language has been tied to the identity of a people. State, people, and language are knotted together, presupposing one another in a mutual set of dependencies. Yet stateless people, such as the Romani, trouble this knot. From the perspective of governmentality and the State, they do not qualify as a "people" nor do they have a "language." Instead they have only a jargon. The historical remedy to the perplexing status of the Romani people and their so-called jargon is to either (a) exclude them from political and social recognition or (b) erase their jargon through national language and grammar. The first strategy has led to erasure while the second to assimilation. Yet Agamben argues that there is a third option: suspending grammar and thus return *all* languages to their origin in jargon or babble, revealing how the ethnic biases against the Romani as somehow lacking language actually reveal how no people *have* language. Thus, babble is not the exception but the rule—a linguistic experience of infancy that remains active in all languages despite attempts to rigorously separate *phone* from *logos* through the institutionalization and standardization of grammar. The model here is Dante, who presented all languages as babble or *vulgare illustre*. But this would also mean that all people are Romani, without a destiny, an identity, a language, and without a nation. According to Agamben, this is not a negative state of being but rather liberatory in that "languages are the jargons that hide the pure experience of language."[13] The task at hand is not transforming jargon/babble into grammars or territorializes peoples into state-bounded identities (as in a colonialist project). It is rather the opposite: releasing the babbling of language so that it can reveal the potentiality of language to be spoken (its anarchic infancy).

In all three experiences—confronting dead languages, speaking a foreign language one does not understand, and babbling—what is at stake is an experiment with language that attempts to expose communicability without communicating anything beyond itself (such as an identity, an essence, and so forth). It would be incorrect to read these three cases as simply inarticulate speech (nonsense). Indeed, one could not experience the mediality of language (its communicative potentiality) if we only had pure nonsense to work with. The key to understanding Agamben's language experiment is that it happens on the margin of language and nonlanguage, sense and nonsense, *phone* and *logos*. Given that infancy happens in every speech act, the experience of infancy can only be made within the context of meaningful speech/language. Only then can a people experience the margin that is present whenever they speak and take up this margin as containing the potentiality for new use.

As with P4C, in a P4I session, thinking and speaking once again cross paths, but there is a difference. In the community of inquiry, speaking seeks to become rationally transparent so that thought can be thought. And in so doing *speaking disappears*. Thus, speaking falls silent at the very moment when thought appropriates it as a tool to communicate how reasonableness has been learned or is being learned. But in P4I, the emphasis shifts so that speaking can be thought, and as such, does not disappear into the background. Instead of speaking as a means to an end outside of itself (the conveyance of learning), thought finds itself when it falls into the silence of pure speaking (babble). This means that thinking speaking's speakability always returns us to infancy, as a threshold that both separates and joins thought and language. We can hear speaking's speakability when children suddenly say, "Wow, what did I just say?" or "I am not sure I understand what I am saying, but I am saying it anyway!"

Whereas P4C has as its goal the communication of specific kinds of speech, procedures, and grammars, P4I presses up against that which is presupposed by such communication: communicability. And it finds such an ability in the very thing that P4C sees as an obstacle or at least as a problem to be negated through learning certain skills and dispositions: babbling. When students start to babble, the facilitator of the community of inquiry is compelled to intervene in order to keep the dialogue "on track" toward achieving a desired goal: the effective and efficient use of reason—hence Lipman's early interest in organizing speech patterns and instituting philosophical grammars (laws) through dialogue. And yet such a pedagogical desire sutures over the aporia of infancy/communicability too quickly, missing the uniqueness of the experience of infancy and its educational importance within the babbling of the community. By letting idle the movement toward reasonable speech (its recodification in terms of philosophical grammar), the secret of speech (its speakability) is encountered in the form of babbling (speech that does not function by laws so much as exposes us to the potentiality for use). And this is barbarous (profane) as it is infantile (inappropriate).

Community of Infancy and Studious Play

In this section we will argue that P4I engages in a particular kind of activity: studious play. Given the emphasis in traditional P4C on cultivating reasonableness, it is surprising that Lipman also emphasized connections between philosophy and playfulness. With Sharp, he writes, "Children's philosophical practice may take many forms" including the spontaneous "play of ideas."[14] Lipman also argues that intellectual thought is not the opposite of play. Indeed, the intellect offers up "its own forms of play."[15] But a community of inquiry is not mere play. Instead it has its own form of play. While it may have playful qualities, it is also educationally directed toward a specific goal (reasonableness) and guided by a teacher (who offers questions to help the students grow, develop, or progress toward this goal). Just as the kinds of speech in P4C are not mere babble, so too the "work" done in the P4C session is not mere playground gaming around. The free play of ideas encouraged in P4C is structured, as we have indicated previously, by certain procedural and linguistic laws. Play is made operative by aligning it with the laws of learning and the laws of reasonableness.

We agree with Lipman that philosophy and play are *not* binary opposites. But our concern is that his articulation of the two sacrifices the adventure of education, which he also desires to preserve. Taking up his problematic, we hope to redeem adventure through Agamben's concept of studious play, which resists both the ritualized and law-abiding behaviors of everyday life of the classrooms and the excesses of the playground but in such a way that the law of learning is not reinstituted so much as suspended. This suspension of the law of learning (in accordance with the sanctity of reasonableness) enables the adventure of infancy to happen through the babble of P4I. Once again drawing on Agamben's work, we can see how a community of infancy offers an outside space within the space of the classroom: a space where thinking and speaking can meet once again *without sacrifice*. At stake in saving P4C from learning imperatives and measurable outcomes is precisely the preservation of the freedom found in the space and time of studious play that students encounter when they babble.

Agamben argues that play and ritual are two forms of human activity defined in relation to time. According to Agamben, "ritual fixes and *structures* the calendar; play, on the other hand … changes and *destroys* it."[16] Ritual is a process of continual reenactment of predefined and predetermined actions or ways of being. Play, on the other hand, concerns itself with the opening up of time outside of the cyclic nature of the ritual. To take up an object as a toy is to suspend its value and to play with it. Play is a kind of suspension of ends or of predetermined functions that are set by the normative pressures of ritual. As Agamben argues, play opens a "new dimension of use" that "is not limited to abolishing the form of separation in order to regain an uncontaminated use that lies either beyond or before it,"[17] but rather a use that activates through deactivation. Thus for

Agamben, new potentialities are opened up through deactivation within play. Think of a toy: a miniaturized truck, for instance, deactivates the functionality of the truck as a tool for transporting goods and thus opens the form of the truck up to new uses. The form is not negated or destroyed or simply affirmed. Rather the form is decoupled from the function via miniaturization as a tactic of suspension. The resulting toy is an inoperative object that is *truck-like* and can be played with.

Two extremes must be avoided. The first is a collapse of time into what Claude Levi-Strauss would refer to as "cold societies" wherein ritual dominates over play. In this extreme, we reach a truly static society, frozen in time, mummified in a perpetually claustrophobic present. Laws of behavior dominate to the point that human action is negated (as in totalitarian countries). On the other extreme, we have "hot societies" of endless play that trump all rituals and submit them to the rush and excitement of constant invention. On an educational level, we can draw a distinction between the ritualized classrooms of high-stakes testing, which are cold and indifferent and the playground, which is a place of hot events. If one extreme concerns the drudgery of seemingly endless communication of what needs to be learned to pass the test then the other concerns the excitement of continually producing new possibilities without the need to conform to predetermined ends dictated by "adults." One communicates laws and procedures while the other communicates what is potentially new, contingent, and playfully disruptive. One concerns the maintenance of what has been signified as important to know and the other opens a space for the flow of new signifiers. Notice the cut within language that is enacted in this dichotomy: there is a division between sanctified speech (of the classroom) and blasphemy (of the playground). Lipman hopes to somehow articulate the two societies through P4C. The goal is neither ritualized thinking (rote learning) nor spontaneous babble (playground talk not appropriate for classrooms). But what he misses in his articulation is what *underlies* and *supports* both while also not being reducible to either: infantile speech. This is the potentiality that makes possible cold and hot societies. Missing infancy, Lipman turns to the laws of reasonableness to help guide babble back toward what is sanctified. He does not discount the playfulness of speaking or thinking that children engage in. Indeed, he sees it as an important connection between childhood and philosophy, thus acting as a kind of justification for P4C as a practice. Yet in the end, it is precisely the cold laws of reasonableness that dictate what can be heard as speech and how such speech can mature into a well-reasoned, ethical, and democratic life.

Agamben seems to gesture toward another possibility when he points out certain social activities that are neither mere rituals nor mere games, and as such make infancy appear. He writes that funerary and initiation rites "do not entirely fit into either the schema of ritual nor that of play, but seem to partake of both."[18] Another such "ceremony" might also be Agamben's brief comments concerning "studious play." Unlike mere ritual, studious play is not bound to the laws of speaking and thinking, but unlike mere play, what is at stake is not the production of new uses and meanings so much as the potentiality for such uses and meanings making itself present. In Agamben's book *Profanations*, it is not play *as such* that is endorsed. Following his analysis of play, Agamben immediately states the following: "It [profanation] is the sort of use that Benjamin must have had in mind when he wrote of Kafka's *The New Attorney* that the law that is no longer applied but only studied is the gate to justice."[19] Commenting further on Benjamin's reflections on Kafka, Agamben continues:

> In the Kafka essay, the enigmatic image of a law that is studied but no longer practiced corresponds, as a sort of remnant, to the unmasking of mythico-juridical violence effected by pure violence. There is, therefore, still a possible figure of law after its nexus with violence and power has been deposed, but it is a law that no longer has force or application, like the one in which the "new attorney," leafing through "our old books," buries himself in study, or like the one that Foucault may have had in mind when he spoke of a "new law" that has been freed from all discipline and all relation to sovereignty.[20]

Suspended, the book (and its laws and traditions) that is studied is deactivated, no longer in force, and thus open to studious play. In this sense, it is not play but rather the relation between play and study that is most important. Summarizing, Agamben writes, "And this studious play is the passage that allows us to arrive at that justice that one of Benjamin's posthumous fragments defines as state of the world in which the world appears as a good that absolutely cannot be appropriated or made juridical."[21] *Studious play* is therefore neither simply play nor lawful ritual but rather the zone of indistinction that lies between the two, separating and conjoining them. It is a zone of contact wherein ritual and play pass through one another without necessarily merging into a synthetic unity of opposites. Nor does one come to define the other (as in Lipman's model). Rather studious play is a kind of hinge that deactivates both play and ritual long enough so that infancy emerges between them.

On our account, a community of infancy is an example of dialogic studious play with language's potentiality that is made possible in moments of suspension. Rules can suddenly be contemplated, and in such contemplation, their determining function can be suspended. The inoperativity opens the rules up for free use through further studious play. In this sense, studious play is an interruption of the time of ritualized learning that dominates schooling practices today in which thinking and speaking are separated. It also does not simply reunite them by subjecting one (playful babble) to the other (law of reasonableness). Studious play offers a kind of inoperative "time out" from the ritualistic reproduction of speaking as confirmation, explanation, or illustration of learning while at the same time postponing any pronouncement on the fate of what language (now reconstructed according to the grammar of philosophy and the law of reasonableness) ought to be. But it is not the purely spontaneous and unpredictable play of the playground either. If the playground emphasizes continual production of events, P4I concerns itself with the origins (infancy) of such production. In this sense, it is a kind of messianic remnant of education that is neither the chronological time of learning and assessing nor the ludic time of pure events in the playground. The problem with the community of inquiry—as Lipman originally theorized it—is that it parasitically depends upon infancy while disavowing it (it negates the communicability of babble while nevertheless employing such communicability as a resource for its ends), and in this gesture, aligns itself with the time of ritualized learning: skills and dispositions are to be learned for a future function within a democratic society. The risk of interruption is exchanged for yet another progressive instrumentalization of infancy. What is lost is precisely the experience of thinking speakability without any preconceived notion of what this otherwise might be in advance of the more basic and fundamental experience of its own potentiality. In this sense, to experience a community of infancy is precisely to rupture the logic of ritual and play that defines the most extreme polarities of the educational experience today. Studious play differs from learning in that there is no law that can maintain a sense of growth, development, or progress toward something beyond itself (reasonableness). All that remains is a speaking that turns thought toward its own conditions of possibility: infancy.

The Adventure of Thinking Speaking/Speaking Thinking

The studious play that is opened up through the babbling of a community of infancy is also equally an adventure! By speaking that which is (un)speakable (infancy), the community studiously plays with its own potentiality to speak without foundation in a predetermined law. Speaking and thinking without foundation is a true adventure. For Agamben, the modern era has devalued and distorted the original notion of adventure. This modern appropriation reduces adventure to nothing more than an individual who happens to be subjected to a series of externally imposed and seemingly contingent obstacles that must be overcome in order to achieve fame and fortune. Adventure thus takes on the form of something radically external or eccentric to everyday life. According to Agamben, nothing could be further from the intended meaning of adventure in medieval, chivalric poetry (a meaning that, for Agamben, has an underground existence in modern philosophy). Most importantly for our purposes, Agamben highlights the odd ambiguity in the word "adventure," which simultaneously refers to *both* an event and a tale or description of the event. Drawing on definitions offered by Jacob Grimm, Agamben points out how "it is not always easy to distinguish between the event and its transposition into words."[22] The adventure, in this sense, does not chronologically precede the story. The telling constitutes the event *as* event. Through the adventure, which is *simultaneously lived and told*, "life and language merge."[23] The location of the adventure is betwixt and between speech and event. It is in the fissure that divides and conjoins them together. Adventure is paradoxical. Both active (something that is pursued) and passive (something that afflicts), it is that which we resolutely take a stand on but also abandon ourselves to without reservations. The adventure carries us away, takes us up, and in so doing affects us but only insofar as we actively speak it.

The event-side of adventure is always an experience of the advent of language, of speaking. The true event is, as Agamben says, an "event of language."[24] This is precisely why adventure cannot be distinguished from the speech that speaks it. What demands to be said is not a specific content but rather the speakability of speech itself. In Agamben's words, the event as the sayable is "something neither merely linguistic nor merely factual; according to an ancient source, it is in between thought and the thing, speech and the world."[25] The thing of language is "its pure sayability, its happening."[26] One can instantly see how the indeterminacy between event and speech in an adventure gives rise to an experience of infancy. An adventure, to be precise, is an experiment with language that enables the event of speaking to be thought through speech. As such, it reconnects thought and speech but in such a way that speech is not reduced to a mere instrument of thought articulating itself.

The subject of adventure has shifted over time. It begins with the medieval knight, who is replaced by the artist. The artist is then eclipsed by the philosopher, or perhaps the poetic philosopher. The quintessential example of the latter is, of course, Heidegger, and his theory of *Ereignis*, which Agamben translates as adventure. The intricacies of Agamben's argument do not concern us here, rather, what we would like to emphasize is how this turn to philosophy opens up the space in Agamben's thoughts of adventure for P4I to enter. The babbling of the community is an adventure in infancy. The educational logic of such babbling is studious play with the very speakability of language as such. Such studious play is not merely melancholic but is rather passionately committed to an adventure. It stumbles upon the rules defining its speakability, and in turn, neutralizes them enough to open them up to free use (beyond cursing and blessing).

The adventure of studious play helps us rethink Lipman's characterization of P4C as "following the argument where it leads."[27] This injunction safeguards against teachers predetermining a set destination and encourages participants to set aside their predetermined assumptions and go down the path that inquiry takes them. They must, in a sense, surrender themselves to the quest. Lipman emphasizes that the teacher does not prioritize which argument or which direction students should follow. This emerges from what he refers to as the situation, which has unique qualities characteristic of a particular community. We agree with Lipman, but we want to make a distinction. Direction might emerge from within the community, but in Lipman's model, this direction itself is always guided by a certain *destiny*, which rests on the tried and true laws of reasonableness. The community might choose its own direction but not the laws, which dictate *how* this direction will be pursued. P4I suspends and renders inoperative the laws of destiny, and in so doing, "following the argument where it leads" becomes more adventurous.

P4I and the Mystery of Education

Where does this adventure lead us? Without a destiny to guarantee its course, does adventure have a clear directionality? Adventure is, as Agamben reminds us, something "whose outcome is difficult to predict."[28] Indeed, it resists being oriented toward a definitive end or cognitive closure. Even romantic adventures that seem to be guided by the protagonists' quests for particular objects—such as the Maltese falcon in John Huston's film of the same name or Rosebud the childhood sled in Orson Well's *Citizen Kane*—leave these objects behind, or at least their mysterious auras. At stake in Agamben's various philosophical adventures is not something sacred or mysterious. Instead, it is something simple, profane, and immediate. He writes, "At issue here is not a secret doctrine or a higher science, nor a knowledge that we do not know."²⁹ It is rather our infancy that is behind the adventure. P4I (as an *experimentum linguae*, an experience of language) is the *experimentum educationis* par excellence, in that it leads us right to the inner sanctum of the "mystery" of education, revealing what cannot not be said and yet for this very reason, disappears. In the following passage from *Infancy and History*, Agamben juxtaposes the concepts of "fable/fairy tale" and "mystery" (ritual), to argue that it is not "mystery," as we may think, but rather the fable that "contains the truth of infancy as man's source of origin."³⁰

> This is why it is the fable, something which can only be narrated, and not the mystery, which must not be spoken of, which contains the truth of infancy as man's source of origin. For in the fairy tale man [*sic*] is freed from the mystery's obligation of silence by transforming it into enchantment: it is not participation in a cult of knowledge which renders him speechless, but bewitchment. The silence of the mystery is undergone as a rupture, plunging man [*sic*] back into the pure, mute language of nature; but as a spell, silence must eventually be shattered and conquered.³¹

Applying this passage to P4I and its role in education, we could say that the "mystery" of education is the "cult of knowledge that renders [human/students] speechless." What is important to highlight here is how knowledge (thinking) and speaking are separated from one another. This separation leads to a sense of mystery: speech that cannot know, and thought that cannot speak. Educational equivalents of this situation can be found in the separation of thinking and speaking introduced at the beginning of this chapter (confirmation, explanation, and/or illustration). In such cases, a void is created separating one from the other that must not (or cannot) be spoken of. In education, the teacher's Voice is often the solution to suturing over the gap. But this solution is inadequate, as this Voice merely reinscribes the very negativity, which it is meant to somehow plaster over.

The fable, on the other hand, that "contains the truth of infancy as man's [*sic*] source of origin" stands for P4I as that activity within the school where "man [*sic*] is freed from the mystery's obligation of silence by transforming it into enchantment." That which was unspeakable (language's origin, its infancy) is spoken in the fable. Or more aptly, language's unspeakable infancy cannot *not* be spoken in the fable. The fable is a response to a demand of language. Rather than silence this demand, it passes fully into language, which now exhibits its own potentiality in the form of a fable that has no end, that has no foundation, and that is truly infantile. In this way, the silence that was perceived to be external to language—and thus mysterious—returns to language as its radical interiority. The negative foundations for the mystery are overcome by the advent of a new birth that is purely positive and affirmative, taken up in the adventure of speaking with others in a community of infancy. The passage continues:

> This is why, in the fairy tale, man [sic] is struck dumb, and animals emerge from the pure language of nature in order to speak. Through the temporary confusion of the two spheres, it is the world of the open mouth, of the Indo-European root *bha (from which the word fable is derived), which the fairy tale validates, against the world of the closed mouth, of the root *mu.[32]

Like the fable and the fairy tale, P4I allows for an experience of infancy that is between animal *phone* and human *logos* without sacrificing either. It is a state where speaking knows itself through its origin in nonspeaking, and where knowledge only speaks itself through the non-knowledge of babble. The indistinction that holds the two poles together is a place of studious play and of adventurous experimentation.

Perhaps we can return here to Lipman's "children's novel" *Pixie*. As pointed out in the introduction to this chapter, *Pixie* can be read as an adventure that, in the end, discovers language. While the main focus of the novel concerns the main character, Pixie, and her exploration of logical, social, familial, aesthetic, causal, and mathematical relationships is the relationship between another character, Brian, and language that is most interesting to us. In the novel, Brian might have stopped talking to other human beings, but he did not stop talking to animals. Indeed, through his experience with a giraffe during a trip to a zoo, Brian discovers speech once again—not how to properly speak but rather speech itself. As such, *Pixie* is a fable focused on the point of infancy that separates and conjoins humans and nonhuman animals. The zoo in the story becomes a kind of crib for cultivating Brian's sense of infancy, or the speakability of speech that only comes through contact with (rather than sacrifice of) the *phone* of other nonhuman animals around him. His silence is therefore not negative but rather positive. It is not meant for human ears; it is a kind of babble that exists between humans and animals without being reducible to either. Furthermore, Brian's silence does not simply disappear once he begins speaking with fellow students. Silence remains within speech, returning it to its origin in infancy. While Pixie, the character, is offered as a model of philosophical inquiry by Lipman, it is to Brian that we must turn in order to get a sense of the real adventure at stake in philosophy. In fact, Pixie's loss of infancy is proportional to her fascination with the increasing mystery of thinking. This mystery shrouds the more basic and fundamental experience of language that Brian hits upon. In short, *Pixie* is, philosophically speaking, a fabulous adventure (rather than a novel).

This adventure is not motivated by a mystery. Indeed, there is no secret that Brian discovers. There is nothing to be learned (no skills or values to be cultivated). Instead, there is only exposure to that which is closest yet easiest to forget: infancy or speakability. Infancy returns thought to language and language to thought without sacrificing one for the other. Through fables, through parables, through babble, this infancy makes itself present in speech and thus available for studious play. What is the directionality of the adventure of P4I? Where does it lead when it has no destiny? Nowhere but to itself. Lipman's characterization of adventure as containing at its heart a mystery turns out to be nothing other than speaking's infancy (which is not much of a mystery after all). The "secret" of one's life intimated by Lipman is not a deep essence encapsulated within a dream that must be excavated through heroic pursuit, but rather glides on the surface of language (through the manner of our speaking) as a constant reminder that the risk of adventure is never far from home, but is rather found in the smallest and most intimate of places (cribs, for instance).

Adventure and Love

Agamben points out that "the one who ventures into the event undoubtedly loves, trembles, and is moved."[33] Love and adventure cross paths: both are active and passive and both are locked within the rhythmic sway between pursuit and abandonment. Thinking and speaking are able to become erotically entwined without sacrificing one for the other. This is an adventure in thinking as much as it is an adventure in speaking. It is important to remember that the origin of adventure is found in chivalric poetry. How does philosophy—and P4I—take up this chivalric origin? How does it find love, without mystery and without sanctity, in and through babbling study and studious play? Get ready for an adventure.

4

Love

What about Love?

While outlining the essential features of a community of inquiry, Lipman makes the following observation of what unfolds during a P4C session:

> Yong children are often found to bond together in intense but inarticulate friendships. Some teachers are inclined to find such classroom friendships a bit threatening to their authority, with the result that they adopt a divide-and-rule strategy. However, classroom communities and friendships should be defined and understood in such a way that no intensification of the one should be perceived as a threat to the other.[1]

What is the nature of these "intense" and "threatening" bonds between students? And what about the teacher? Is the teacher left out of the bonds and thus left in the position of outsider? Lipman does not specify further, but we would like to call them love bonds. What is love if not a friendship that is intense yet inarticulate? Perhaps Lipman wanted to shy away from the language of love because it is either (a) too clichéd or (b) it is too easily given over to sexual connotations. Or perhaps it was simply too far afield of education to even be considered as an educational concept—let alone an educational concept germane to P4C. Indeed, love is not the first thing that comes to mind when we think of education (or educational philosophy, for that matter). And yet when we think of our own school days, it is some form of love we are most likely to remember—be it the crush on another student, the admiration for our favorite teacher, the passion we developed for a particular subject, or the memories of intense relationships we have with others when we are involved in shared inquiry (as Lipman points out). Love is also frequently evoked (by students and teachers alike), as the ultimate endorsement/validation ("I love Ms. K.!" "I love Math!" "Mr. P. loves me!", "I just love that kid!").

Looking back over the broad scope of philosophy of education, love does (or should) play an essential role in education (and pedagogy, in particular).

The idea of love has been proposed by a wide range of thinkers with various noncritical, critical, and post-critical perspectives on education, including Plato, Paulo Freire, bell hooks, Peter McLaren, Antonia Darder, and Joris Vlieghe and Piotr Zamojski.[2] But most importantly for us, it is David Kennedy's analysis of the five kinds of community in P4C where love is defined as one of the essential structural dimensions of a community of inquiry.[3] As such, Kennedy enables us to name the intense yet inarticulate relationship between students (and perhaps teachers!) that Lipman gestures to above. For Kennedy, the love of the community of inquiry includes erotic and agapic dimensions. It is odd that he does not include philia (brotherly love), which seems to be the kind highlighted by Lipman, but nevertheless, Kennedy is to be commended for at least recognizing the important role of love (in its many forms) in defining P4C. Indeed, Kennedy argues that love is what enables the community to "come together" in a "telos" leading toward "unity on a somatic level."[4] Love is part of a teleological structure that necessarily directs the community toward a harmonious unity as its destiny. It is this utopian ideal that motivates students to continue to dialogue, work through differences, and strive for mutual recognition. Of course, there are dangers of "false harmony," which for Kennedy, is merely self-love in disguise, but love, in the strong sense, is the force that can overcome this false harmony (as long as the practitioners continue the struggle). The embrace of the whole community is not antithetical to reasonableness. Instead, Kennedy argues that love is indeed reasonable and thus complements the larger telos of P4C: Lipman's notion of a "well-tempered life."[5]

In this chapter, we want to inquire further into the theme of love. But to do so will mean suspending the *functionality* of love as it is discussed in P4C. When love is given an internal telos or necessary destiny of its own (harmony in mutual recognition) it loses what is most lovely about love: the joy of whatever someone is in their difference. It is not an attempt to overcome or sublate these differences into unity, but rather an appreciation for whatever differences there are. Love, on our reading, has no function, but only use. It has nothing to teach us, there is nothing to learn from love. Instead, through love we are exposed to whatever we are, and thus open up to the use of ourselves by ourselves and others in the form of studious play.

In this sense, our chapter has two major goals. First, we wish to foreground the need to think of love in terms of the educational problematic of potentiality. While many facets of love have been covered by the aforementioned authors, none of them directly address love in relation to what is actual versus what is in potential (within a student, a subject, a practice, a world, and so on). This will be an ontological interpretation of love rather than an emotive or somatic one. In particular, this means making a distinction between love as *having* (a potential or actual identity as *x* kind of person) and love as *being* whatever. We will discuss love as having and being in relation to the self and to others in the P4I community, illustrating how they are interconnected. Second, we hope to further theorize P4I as a practice by foregrounding the importance and uniqueness that love plays. Whereas P4C focuses on education as a means to an end (the cultivation of specific, predetermined thinking, civic, and ethical skills to lead a particular kind of life), P4I focuses on education as a pure means (without success conditions orienting it this way or that). Because of this, P4I is no longer about cultivating philosophical styles or speaking in the name of a greater harmony or unity to come. Rather, it is about seeing what is philosophical in an existing manner of speaking and loving whatever manner this is as a manifestation of infancy.

But before we turn to our reconstruction of love, we want to clear some ground by suggesting two modes of loving and being loved that are prevalent in educational practices and discourses today: tough love and love actually. These are modes of love that circulate throughout the learning society and, we assume, can be found in any number of pedagogical approaches, including variants of P4C. Again, our goal is not emotive or somatic but rather ontological, pinpointing how different kinds of love imply different models of the relationship between potentiality and actuality, means and ends. The problem with the first two models is that they are ultimately predicated on some form of sacrifice (negation) that transforms an oath into a curse, love into hate. As an alternative, we offer the concept "whatever love," where one can finally allow one's self to be whatever one is (in one's mannerisms) without cursing or blessing one's identity and accept whatever others are as a manifestation of a singular existence in which infancy constitutes itself. And in this sense, we will provide a new justification for a purely affirmative love in education.[6]

Tough Love: "I Love You for What You Can and Should Become"

Given the current educational climate of high-stakes testing, accountability, and efficiency, we may wonder: Where is the love? But maybe the problem is not so much the lack of love, but that what we encounter in the high-stakes classroom is mainly the "tough love" variety of the teacher pushing students to succeed.

Tough love is of course not a new phenomenon in education. In fact, it could be considered the hallmark of traditional conceptions of education, if by "tough love" we mean making someone do things against their will with the justification that it is for their own good in the long run ("You will thank me later!"). In a traditional educational setting, the justification for the treatment of students consists in the assumption that the teacher (as the representative of the school and the educational establishment more generally) knows what's good for the students based on some ultimate truth about the world/human nature—whether it is beholding the idea of the good (Plato), realizing the students' nature as rational beings (Rousseau, Kant), or their self-realization in accordance with the universal spirit (Hegel). What all conceptions of education that operate with a preconceived goal based on some universal truth have in common is that the love of the teacher is not directed at something the student *is*, but at what the student can and ought to be in the future. Students, in this model, who repeat the oath of the teacher, likewise fall in love with their future selves. But, as with all oaths, this also demands a certain curse over the present sense of self as inadequate, lacking, and needing to be developed further.

Even Paulo Freire's oft-cited view of love fits into this category. Although Freire is clear that the teacher does not lead the students, that the oppressed must liberate themselves, and that knowledge should not be given to the oppressed, nevertheless, there is a sense that Freire advocates a form of tough love that puts him within the philosophical lineage outlined above. For instance, Freire argues that the oppressed suffer from narration sickness precisely because they are "under the sway of magic and myth" that leads them to "imitate" the oppressors.[7] And imitation culminates in "self-depreciation" and "fatalism."[8] Because of this internalization process, the oppressed will have a certain psychological resistance to change and transformation—hence Freire's insistence on the importance of teacher authority just as much as on student freedom. To underemphasize authority is to overly romanticize Freire's critical pedagogy and the willingness of the oppressed to spontaneously liberate themselves.[9] For Freire there is always a "fear of freedom"[10] that has to be overcome. Guiding the authority of the teacher is his or her knowledge of the ontological vocation of the human and a utopian hope "for the quest for human completion."[11] Thus there is a subtle theory of human potentiality at work in Freire's pedagogy, one that emphasizes the negation of what is so as to actualize what ought to be in the future. And this process is guided by the tough love of the teacher who must help the oppressed overcome their fear of freedom and their resistance to transformation by continually orienting them back to the ontological truth of human existence (as Freire sees it).

On this model, what is loved is the potentiality to become a specific kind of human being (according to an ontological vocation). The role of the teacher or facilitator is to pinpoint this potentiality and then act as its shepherd, keeping potentiality on track so that it can actualize itself sometime in a future state. The smooth transition from potentiality to actuality is what is emphasized. Potentiality must *exhaust* itself in a form of actualization so that the change of state can be assessed accurately. Notice, for instance, Freire's emphasis on human *completion*. Educational success rests upon the movement of what is in potentiality (yet repressed by the fear of freedom) toward actualization. But here is the Agambenian worry: what is sacrificed is precisely one's *impotentiality* or one's ability to not be. Indeed, within tough love, this is precisely what is the internal obstacle to achieving completion of the human. For Freire, impotentiality might be cast in a negative light as fear of freedom, but in more common, everyday educational parlance, we might also think of it in terms of a lack of willpower, attentiveness, urgency, resilience, or an overabundance of procrastination or laziness. These are all ways in which the ability to *not* do or be might be reduced to a negative state that must be overcome through *tough love* that steps in and acts as a willful supplement to the student's perceived lack.

But if the love of the teacher is not directed at what the student *is*, it is not really directed at the student at all, because the student is not (yet)—and may in fact never be—what the teacher wants him or her to become. Rather, loving the student for what the teacher wants her to become means loving the student not for what she is, but rather for her ability to realize something that *the teacher* considers to be valuable, that is, *her* ideal of what it means to be a good, educated, successful (etc.) person (or as Freire would argue, what it means to be a complete human). So, it is the teacher's love of their ideal that makes them "love" the student as someone who can help them realize that ideal. Walter Omar Kohan expresses this point well when he writes that in Plato's conception of education "children represent adults' opportunity to carry out their ideals."[12] In other words, the student is "loved" as an instrument, a means to an end. And to the extent to which the ideal is something that the teacher—presumably—embraces and embodies themselves—it may actually be more accurate to describe this as a form of self-love ("I love you because you will become what I am and what I love, and love about myself"). Hence the danger of tough love: in the name of potentiality, the potentiality (and its co-constituting relationship with impotentiality) is sacrificed.

This becomes even more apparent in the discourse of P4C where the teacher loves the community *in so far* as it approximates the ideal of reasonableness.

The teacher knows in advance where the community ought to head (deliberative democracy as the ultimate good) and relies on this knowledge to assess their improvement over time. The teacher looks for and listens for certain clues to indicate growth, development, and progress toward achieving certain, predefined aims. And by structuring the community as an intentional learning community, potentiality is submitted to a trial. This trial might be necessary for the students to learn how to become democratic citizens or reasonable subjects, but in so doing there is a danger that infancy itself will be lost. Just as the individual must sacrifice their impotentiality in the quest to actualize a certain ideal, so too the community suffers a similar fate.

The same is no less true in the current educational climate of the learning society, except that instead of some lofty ideal, the ultimate goal of education (equally based on a notion of human nature, only a more reductionist and impoverished one) that serves as the justification for tough love now consists in students fulfilling what is seen as their primary potential: to become successful contributors to the economy. And just like in those other models, the teacher expresses her love by helping students realize what she considers to be worth achieving (e.g., the ability to become lifelong learners who are always cursing themselves). This is the case even if she does not believe in the goal/ideal herself and just sees it as her duty to do what is necessary to make the students able to function/survive in the world as it is (however much she may hate that world). However different the motivation for, or even the quality of her love, may be, the way that love is expressed, and the effect on the students remains the same.

The problem with intentional educational communities (of all varieties, including possible communities of inquiry) is that they might be highly successful in achieving certain goals and outcomes, yet such learning reduces potentiality to a mere means to an end that is predetermined in advance by philosopher kings, by critical pedagogues, or by purported experts. The love expressed in these intentional forms is tough because it forces potentiality to express itself in a particular modality that is deemed socially, educationally, or economically viable, thus sacrificing something that remains in excess of any possible teleological fulfillment of a human nature, productivity matrix, and so on. Perhaps even more troubling is the observation that the potentiality at stake in tough love is not even that of the student but rather that of the teacher who assumes that the potentiality of the student is the *same* as their potentiality. When the student "fails to live up to his or her full potential" then love turns into hate of whatever one has become. The teacher's hope is betrayed, and blessings turn into curses. These curses might be directed at the student for failing, but even then, the ultimate target is a kind of self-cursing directed at the teacher (and their failure to help actualized the assumed potentiality). Such a gesture effectively undermines the very meaning of potentiality to be otherwise than that which can be predicted, prescribed, or predetermined.

Love Actually: "I Love You Just the Way You Are"

Given that traditional approaches and the current educational regime foster a kind of love that is not directed at what the student is, but at something he or she can and ought to become, we may expect to find a different (and more appealing) kind of love in the progressive, child-centered, constructivist classroom that is all about letting students be, putting their interests, desires, and preferences first. If tough love in the traditional classroom is not about who the students are, but who they ought to become in the future (their potentiality to actualize x), love in the progressive classroom—we could call it "love actually"—is all about loving the students for who they are in their immediate actuality.

This approach comes with its own set of problems, though. If we assume that the love of the teacher is directed at who the students are, the question remains how progressive "loving the students for who they are" really is, given that such love might become increasingly oppressive, keeping the student from recognizing that the self is not reducible to a given identity. Can't we imagine a teacher saying, "Why would you want to change? I love you just the way you are!" In this sense, the student becomes trapped because his or her identity becomes a *necessity* ("I *must be* who I am"). In praising identity, there might be an unintended consequence: the fetishization or reification of said identity in the name of acceptance. Belonging to one's self as a property of one's identity ends up commodifying the self, leaving little room for whatever might remain in excess of a given identity. If one changes, then the self becomes unrecognizable to the self and to others. "That is not who you *really* are," says the teacher when her prized student suddenly starts slacking off or diverts interests away from what is expected. "You need to embrace your authentic self, whoever that is!" warns the teacher who sees a student passionate about biology suddenly take a 180-degree turn by majoring in art.

The worry here is that teacherly love becomes wedded to the actual over and above the potentiality of the student. Likewise, when the student repeats the oath of the teacher, loyalty to whomever one is becomes a curse—one is doomed to the necessity of one's identity as an end in and for itself. If there is deviation from this authentic core or necessary essence, one can only hate one's self for the betrayal. Thus, love turns into hate, and we once again find ourselves in a cycle of negation. In the community of inquiry, love actually amounts to nothing more than praising/blessing the group for its works and its deeds. "Good job today!" or "The dialogue was really excellent!" The oath of the teacher holds the community hostage to a judgment that is delivered from outside itself—offering reinforcement through the Voice of the teacher. The problem here is that such reinforcement guides students away from an experience of their own speech as such back toward the Voice of the teacher (and their ability to bless and curse at the students).

To summarize: While tough love has the problem of being about what the students *are not*, but rather about their potentiality to actualize, in the future, whatever it is the teacher believes to be worth actualizing, the love actually variety has the opposite problem. Here the teacher—assuming the students are really the object of his or her love—loves the students *only* for who they are, that is, their pure actuality, their definable identities as this or that kind of person with this or that set of interests, skills, and dispositions. Tough love concerns a future actualization of a present potentiality whereas love actually concerns pure actuality as such, without remainder. The first views students as a means to an end (predetermined by the teacher and their love interests) while the second reduces the child to an end (as exhausted by what the child's interests, behaviors, and competencies are). In other words, in both cases what is sacrificed is whatever the students are as a pure means (undetermined by the teacher). The dialectic of oath and curse sets in, and love becomes an act of policing the self and others in a community.

Whatever Love: "I Love You for Being *Whatever*"

What we suggest here is that another kind of love in education is possible that transcends the dichotomy of either loving the students only for their potential to actualize an identity the teacher wants them to actualize (tough love), or loving them for whomever they are, in its fullness, completeness, and necessity (love actually). To conceptualize such a truly different kind of love in education, we enlist once again the help of Agamben in order to theorize what we are calling whatever love. And for an example of an educational practice that features this kind of love, we look at the P4I practice.

Briefly summarized, Agamben argues that "[l]ove is never directed toward this or that property of the loved one (being blond, being small, being tender, being lame), but neither does it neglect the properties in favor of an insipid generality (universal love). The lover wants the loved one *with all of its predicates, its being such as it is*."[13] Agamben continues, "Whatever singularity has no identity. It is not determinate with respect to a concept, but neither is it simply indeterminate; rather it is determined only through its relation to … the totality of its possibilities."[14] Another way of saying this is that a lover loves whatever a person is. Whatever is a philosophical concept in Agamben's work intimately linked to the question of potentiality. Whereas the history of philosophy has often submitted potentiality (the ability to) to actuality (what has been done), Agamben wants to think potentiality without sacrifice, without negation. When potentiality is absorbed into actuality without remainder, impotentiality (the ability not to) is sacrificed, or it is experienced only in and through its privation. Yet Agamben argues that there is another possibility opened up by Aristotle's thinking that forces us to reconceptualize the instrumental relationship between potentiality and actuality. Here Agamben is worth quoting in full:

> Of the two modes in which, according to Aristotle, every potentiality is articulated, the decisive one is that which the philosopher calls "the potentiality to not-be" (*dynamis me einai*) or also impotence (*adynamia*). For if it is true that whatever being always has a potentiality character, it is equally certain that it is not capable of only this or that specific act, nor is it therefore simply incapable, lacking in power, nor even less is it indifferently capable of everything, all powerful: The being that is properly whatever is able to not-be; is capable of its own impotence.[15]

Being whatever does not mean the being that is capable of anything and everything under the sun. This would be the lie of capitalistic hubris: dream big and you can achieve anything you want! But also, whatever being is not reducible to simply those acts that one can do ("this is who I am and I am not going to change!") or the identity that one has ("I am the kind of person that has x skill and x interests"). Indeed, whatever is precisely what escapes representation as a predicate of a subject's "identity" and escapes one's abilities to "act" (as willful expressions of one's identity). Whatever is paradoxical: it is so personal that it is impersonal (escaping the boundaries of an identity), and it is so passive that it is active (in that it is an actualization of an impotence).

This last point is particularly difficult to grasp. Whatever being is not simply impotence: I can't do that! Instead, whatever being is a kind of being that is *capable* of its own impotence, of its impotentiality. But what does this mean? For Agamben, it would mean that the passage from potentiality to actuality would not sacrifice impotentiality but rather manifest it. This is not a simple transition from potentiality to act. Agamben summarizes, "If every power is equally the power to be and the power to not-be, the passage to action can only come about by transporting (Aristotle says 'saving') in the act its own power to not-be."[16] To be whatever one is means that one displays impotentiality in their acts (thus deactivating these acts in the moment of their actualization). *One cannot not be whatever one is*. "I cannot not be whoever I am" is different from saying either (a) "I am different from who I am (my true potentiality will be realized in a future moment)" or (b) "I have to be who I am (as this is my essence or true identity)." The point (a) sacrifices the sufficiency of the present for a possible future. It is always oriented away from itself in order to find itself. When schools say, "Come here and learn to fulfill your true potentiality" or when critical pedagogues say, "Learn this and you will be emancipated in the future," or when P4C practitioners say, "You will be prepared to be a democratic citizen through P4C"; they are turning potentiality into a means to an end, and thus sacrificing its relation to the impotentiality of the present. The point (b) is also problematic from the perspective of impotentiality. When teachers say, "You are perfect the way you are" or "Don't change," they are exhausting potentiality into an actuality without remainder, again sacrificing impotentiality. Whatever being is a being that is not oriented away from itself toward a future. Nor is it an essence or truth or authentic core that has to be embraced without cursing the self (in the form of a betrayal). If tough love curses the self, then love actually blesses the self as the identity that must actualize it. In both cases, we are in the terrain of oath taking and oath receiving by the teacher. But whatever being is *contingently sufficient and necessary*, meaning one can be whatever one is without destiny and without necessity. This is a mode of being that cannot be blessed or cursed as we are simply abandoned to it.

Indeed, for Agamben, whatever is precisely an "inessential supplement" or what he refers to as a halo that is "added to perfection—something like a vibration of that which is perfect, the glow at its edges."[17] In other words, whatever as a halo is a displacement of the edges of something, or a supplement that is not a property but also not beyond the properties of a subject. It is a vibration at the edge of properties that lights up these properties while also destabilizing them, somehow adding nothing to perfection while at the same time transforming it completely. In short, whatever we are is only accessed through the identity we have (our predicates) while also not reducible to that identity. Instead, whatever we are is an "event of an outside."[18] It is not a property as such but a vibration (an event) that happens to properties in their perfection that pushes these properties to their (im)proper dissolve. Stated differently, whatever pushes properties to the limit of their representability and, in turn, pushes identity beyond itself to its proverbial outside. As an event, whatever is never something we have (as in an identity) but rather something that we experience in the way our being appears to us. The subject becomes *singular* in its being and thus no longer fits nicely within any class or type of person. And what is most peculiar is that whatever we are appears to be the most *insignificant* supplement to this mode of being. It is a kind of frivolous excess above and beyond our "perfection." It is therefore exposed through our ticks, quirks, idiosyncrasies—those things we don't claim as our own or cannot identity ourselves with. The event of our whatever being is not claimed as our destiny or as our "truth," instead it is discounted as an irrelevant and meaningless accident or inconsequential nothing. It is a happening that barely happens.

Another way to concretize this concept is through Agamben's discussion of manner. In *Profanations*, Agamben discusses style versus manner. Style is a habit that has become necessary and relatively fixed. It is, in a sense, a constitutive dimension of identity, or the elemental building block that enables identity to be represented as a particular kind of having. Manner brings style to life through a vibration (an inessential and insignificant event). One cannot live a style without manner, even if manner escapes the style that it brings into existence. Manner exposes itself in subtle gestures that fall below the radar of conscious oversight or ritualized habituation, and as such is precisely that which is not claimed as part of one's identity. Manners reveal one's whatever being in that one cannot-not exhibit them. They are impotential events (or passive events) that an individual can only yield to, or surrender to without reservation. These manners stylize style as a supplement to perfection.

In surrendering to our manners, we accept whatever we are as sufficient. This does not mean that the manner expresses an essence or an authentic self. Instead, they are inessential surpluses that always seem to escape us or embarrass us when someone else points them out (as they are *more* than what can be described or represented as a style, and also somehow *less* than the prescriptions of a style). They are not recognizable traits of a true self in its full actuality or of a skill in its optimal operability but rather vibrations at the farthest edges of identity that destabilize identity by overfilling it or interruptions of operability at the point of is maximal actualization. For Agamben, whatever is a "singularity plus an empty place."[19] It is, stated differently, the exposure of identity to what is beyond it (beyond any sense of having). Or, we might say that whatever is the indeterminating surplus at the limit of any determination (of something *as* the kind of thing that it is). The resulting shutter or vibration always introduces a contingency into any necessity, destabilizing what is necessary, even if by only a fraction of a fraction. Indeed, this vibration must, as Agamben clearly states, be *beyond* representation, measure, or capture. In this way, whateverness ensures each individual cannot be transformed into a caricature or stereotype and, as such, opens a space for what is most singular (or what can never be turned into a property) in each person. This impotential, minor, fragile excess (that we cannot not be) does not retreat from actualization or exhaust itself in actualization but rather makes itself felt within any given actualization as a manner.

Manners are inappropriable, meaning they cannot be transformed into a property of self or other. They are not something someone has. They are, as Agamben argues,[20] paradoxical in that we are simultaneously consigned to them while not being able to assume them. They are so proper to a singular being that they are improper, meaning that we cannot identify them as representing who we are. Instead, they merely testify *that* we are in our singularity. Summarizing, Agamben writes, style is "disappropriating appropriation (a sublime negligence, a forgetting oneself in the proper)" while manner is "an appropriating disappropriation (a presenting oneself or remembering oneself in the improper)."[21] Style, in other words, is a loss of the self in a habit that one has (that properly *belongs* to the self) whereas manner finds the self in precisely that which the self does not have (the event of yielding to an outside).

Manner also helps us understand how the demand of existence (ontologically speaking) is experienced by an individual. The demand of being cannot be experienced *in general* but only singularly. Manner is the way the demand to live exposes itself through an "infinite series of modal oscillations."[22] The paradox here is intentional: the necessity of being (demand) is only lived through the contingencies of singular oscillations, or tiny, insignificant events. Agamben summarizes, "[F]orm-of-life is the 'manner of rising forth,' not a being that has this or that property or quality but a being that is its mode of being, which is its welling up and is continually generated by its 'manner' of being."[23] Manner generates a form-of-life by vibrating the edges of a habituated style in such a way that it exposes the demand to be (to exist) in a singular mode of rising forth that is irreducible to any preconstituted style/habit. If, as Agamben argues, mannerisms form our form-of-life out of the demand of/for being, then we might add to this and suggest that infantile babble is a form-of-speaking that responds to the demand of language.

The example that Agamben gives of whatever being is the pianist Glenn Gould. First, we might think that Gould is a genius who is defined by the property of having certain perfected skills. But Agamben proposes a really different reading of Gould. Gould does not will his genius to manifest itself in his playing, instead, he simply allows himself to not not-play. He is radically passive. He yields to playing because it is his passion, meaning his affliction.

Gould was not in control of his manner but rather exposes himself fully through his mannerisms (such as humming, directing with his left hand while playing with his right hand, and so forth). Being asked whether he would change any of these mannerisms if he could, he responded: "No, if I didn't do that there would be an absolute deterioration in my playing. That is an indispensable component."[24] He is not in control, rather he has abandoned himself to whatever is beyond his identity on the inside of his identity (his manner). The exposure of the self to the event of its outside (its manner of being whatever it is) gives Gould's music a certain halo, or singularity that cannot be fully represented or easily imitated. Indeed, if Gould's performance could be reduced to nothing more than a talent or a skill, then it would not have its singular halo and could therefore be easily imitated. As Jeremy Siepmann states, "He [Gould] has driven me time and again to go back to the score and learn from it afresh—not in emulation of Gould, whose most extreme mannerisms remain both inimitable and undesirable—but in search of renewed contact with the spirit and the endless fascination of the music itself."[25]

Manner, as argued above, is how one "exposes" one's self to an outside. Agamben also describes this exposure as the "free use of the self"[26] where we are *generated* through our manner of being. These mannerisms constitute a self through how it lives without comparing itself to something transcending its mode of living (such as a norm or law, or notion of salvation, or curse or blessing). The result of free use of the self is not a new creation *ex nihilo* nor a more effective or more authentic self but simply whatever the self is through its use of itself via its faculties. The paradox here should not be underestimated: the act of creating a mode of being is radically passive and seemingly inessential; it is an event of yielding to whatever one cannot not be. A self is radically poor in its having to be, and this poverty is only matched by its impotence (its ability to not not be whatever it is in response to a demand). For this reason, whatever being is perfectly finite rather than infinitely pliable and flexible. Think of Gould: he is whatever he is absolutely through the event of yielding to an impotentiality (an ability to not not-play in the face of the demand of music). His being exposes itself through the insignificant surplus added to the perfection of his skills that stylizes his style.

We might say that Gould *learned* how to play the piano through his willfully directed desire. Perhaps tough love of his teachers pushed him forward toward the actualization of his essence as a "genius." But his genius is not found in the skills he has learned. Without reservation, he yields to his mannerism with a certain kind of abandonment, and this is something done over and above any will. Indeed, mannerism is precisely the event of the outside, meaning it is beyond the will to direct it. Instead, it is an eclipse of the will by that which is weakest and most poor: impotentiality to not not-respond to the demand of music.

To love is precisely to love this enigmatic whatever, this inability to not be that exposes itself in our manners and in our infancy. This means that whatever love is without oath taking, and by extension, without curse making. To use Agamben's terminology, whatever love is "irreparable"[27] or a love that separates itself from any ethic of saving (the self or the other). Whatever love is not about salvation. It has no missionary zeal to it. Rather it merely accepts as sufficient that the self is unable not to yield to whatever demand exerts itself on its being. In this sense it is a *profane* kind of love, a love of that which is most improper about a self (love for an inessential, if not obscene or exaggerated surplus). This also means that whatever love is radically *unconditional*. Both tough love and love actually have specific conditions that must be met for their love to express itself. In tough love, potentiality *must* actualize itself in a foreseeable future in a way that can be identified as proper. This is tough because the current identity must be cursed as somehow fallen, distorted, alienated, immature, and irrational. In love actually, an identity that a self has must be preserved through a blessing. In both cases, there are conditions that must be met for love (as an oath) to be given. Yet with whatever love, there are no such conditions. Whatever inessential and contingent supplement that defines the event of being is sufficient for love.

In linguistics, there is a peculiar phrase called a nominal syntagma. Such a phrase is a complete assertion but does not contain a verbal predicate. It is therefore wrong to translate ancient phrases such as "the water best" to "the water is best." The latter, for Agamben, conceals the uniqueness of the nominal syntagma, which does not utilize a copula (is) to conjoin subject and predicate. Such an issue bears philosophical meaning for Agamben. Whereas "to be" in Western language often refers to either existential meaning (positing the existence of something) or predicative meaning (positing the having of certain essences or features), the nominal syntagma "escapes the distinction, presenting a third type irreducible to the two other types."[28] As an example of the nominal syntagma, Agamben then turns to love. Summarizing, Agamben writes, "Love does not allow for copulative predication, it never has a quality or an essence as its object."²⁹ The minute love is reduced to a set of predicates as in "I love him/her because she is x, y, and z" then love ceases to be love. Instead of loving the person, we come to desire only his/her particular set of attributes (a certain identity that the person *must have* as a precondition for love) as conditions justifying love. Hence, when those attributes are missing, then we can stop "loving" the person. But when someone says "I love beautiful so-and-so" what is meant is not simply that so-and-so IS beautiful (they have the quality of beauty as expressed in and through x, y, or z predicates). The individual loves so-and-so's being whatever that being is as beautiful.

Here we can conclude somewhat schematically with several arguments we have outlined here:

1. Tough love privileges potentiality over actuality.
2. Love actually privileges actuality over potentiality.
3. Whatever love privileges the paradoxical contact between impotentiality and actuality through impotential acts (and thus does not involve sacrifice).
4. Whereas the first two have conditions that justify love, the third is unconditional and thus truly improper and profane.

Lovely Friendship

But whatever love is not simply about the self and its potentiality. Think here of Gould once again. Gould exposes whatever he is when he plays (or when he yields to the demand of music through his mannerisms). Indeed, the very notion of whatever as an event of the outside indicates a point of contact between interior and exterior, self and other, that inherently lends itself to questions of community, or, as the case might be, friends. As Agamben argues, friendship is not about recognizing sameness or achieving holistic unity (as in Kennedy's model) but rather about mutually exposing whatever, of being radically nude in front of one another. To develop this point further, we need to distinguish between Agamben's notion of love and friendship. Whereas Agamben's notion of love refers to the particular relationship of the individual members of the community to each other (and to themselves), his notion of friendship should be understood as a fundamental ontological state or mode of being. Like other key concepts in his work, Agamben derives his idea of friendship from Aristotle. In the *Nicomachean Ethics*, Aristotle writes that recognizing someone as a friend is to not recognize him or her as "something," and that "friendship is neither a property nor a quality of a subject."[30] For Agamben, this passage contains "the ontological basis of Aristotle's theory of friendship."[31] By "ontological basis" he means what Aristotle describes as a "sensation of pure being," (calling it "in itself sweet"), that is, the very sensation of being alive. For Aristotle, this sensation (of pure being, existence, life) can be experienced jointly with another person. "Friendship," Agamben writes, "is the instance of this 'con-sentiment' of the existence of the friend within the sentiment of existence itself."[32] Rather than merely denoting the relationship between two distinct subjects (or becoming one in a holistic unity/erasing all differences between two selves), Agamben points out that, for Aristotle, the friend is a "*heteros autos*" (another self), due to the fact that friends see each other as singularities who are their manners (rather than identities that have characteristic properties). While this is very similar to Agamben's notion of love, friendship places emphasis on the particular ontological state (i.e., a mode of being) made possible by a "desubjectification," that is, a becoming other than the self, "at the very heart of the most intimate sensation of the self."[33] It is in this sense that he writes: "Friends do not share something (birth, law, place, taste): they are shared by the experience of friendship" given that "what has to be shared is the very fact of existence, life itself."[34] Remember, whatever being is an event of the outside within the inside of the self. It turns the self as itself into the self as other. Because of this, friendship is a contact point of two empty spaces on the very edge of identity—the vibrating, indeterminating mannerisms that are not properties of a subject so much as events of desubjectification (im) proper to the subject. Sharing existence between friends is therefore never a way of sharing the constitutive properties of two identities united together. Instead, it is the sharing of the empty space of sharing where identity dissolves through the vibrations of manner in the face of a demand.

Adding to what has been said earlier about love as a particular way of relating to both oneself and another person, and about the role of love in the P4I community, we can now say that the beloved, as friend, is not another I (an identifiable subject) but rather is another self (a *heteros autos*) in the sense that he or she is, like I, in a state of indeterminacy (infancy, impotentiality), making him or her, like me, a living possibility to be a singularity through the manner of their being affected. It is only by communally dwelling on the margin between pure being/voice and speech/language/truth that being (and language) can be sensed: "Language opens the possibility of not-being, but at the same time it also opens a stronger possibility: existence, that something is."[35] In other words, at the level of language, the intentional community allows for the experience of love between the members of the classroom community, while, at an ontological level, this allows for the experience of friendship as a communal experience of being as a sharing of language.

What makes this possible is that—due to the demand exposed by the teacher—the students do not see each other in relation to something that transcends the community as what determines how they relate to each other. With the absence of the Voice of the teacher (representing authority, truth), the students can meet as friends and love one another's whatever. By silencing the Voice of the teacher, he or she opens up a space and time for love and friendship between and among the students as they share the sharing of a demand of language as what is most basic and common. Rather than being defined by external ends (specific educational outcomes), the community of infancy is defined by the experience of love and friendship, or, in Agamben terms, as neither a means to an end nor an end in itself, but as a means without end.

In P4I, students experience their infancy precisely by their *inability to not speak*. This exposes itself through manners. These manners cannot be organized into evidence of increasing levels of reasonability or somatic harmony/unity. Instead, they continually interrupt such teleological goals with a flourish of excitement and love that overflows the ability to measure or quantify or assess. One cannot not speak in P4I, even if this is through subtle gestures or quiet mannerisms. The community has no power to prevent speaking and therefore is maximally weak and impotent before the demand of language. But by being so weak, it truly *loves* whatever the community ends up being without reserve and without conditions. This is a community of friends—not of individuals who mirror one another, but friends who love through whatever emerges in terms of singular mannerisms (singular forms-of-life) and through the rules the community uses to constitute itself in its differences.

This last point brings up another important distinction between types of educational love. Whatever love is radically *indifferent*. Tough love and love actually are—on our reading—about being deeply involved in the lives of students. Tough love cares so much for students that it is willing to risk losing students by being so tough, and the second cares so much for maintaining the love relationship that it risks a form of intimacy that might prevent the student from ever challenging themselves to push beyond preset boundaries. But whatever love is totally indifferent to whomever the child is (any form of predetermined identity that is assumed according to biases or prejudices) or what the child will become (any form of teleology of human fulfillment or simple economic survival). Whatever love is only interested in loving a student's manners or those moments of desubjectification or yielding to the event of the outside that nevertheless produce a halo around the student. These manners indicate the singular existence of the child in relation to a demand of existence or a demand of language. They are the way in which identity yields to a form-of-life.

In particular, P4I loves a student's *linguistic* manners, or how the manner of speaking reveals the speakability or communicability of language. This is not a property that anyone has command of. While speakability appears as that which is most intimate to the self (as a speaking being), it is actually what is most improper and external as language only happens to a human being from the outside through learning. And after language is acquired, the speakability of said language remains inappropriable as an excess within yet outside any given utterance. Thus the event of language always remains somehow external to the speaker as an inessential supplement to every act of speaking that can never be owned or claimed by anyone. In this sense, the infancy of language maintains that it is always open to free use through mannerism. In an educational setting, such mannerisms surprise the student's as much as the P4I facilitator. They appear in the event of speaking as the tick or gesture that never belongs within the telos of the community. In this sense, manners are so personal that they become impersonal—shared with others as an empty space that no one can claim as property. Linguistic manners are the speakability of language speaking itself (as an event of an outside) through the inessential vibrations of what is said in its saying. Manners return the members of P4I to the infancy of language's ability to be spoken as that which is improper to anyone and yet shared by all in the community. In P4I whatever love is precisely the circulation of manners through a community that shares with each other what is most inessential, most poor, and most weak in the face of the demand of language.

This brings us to our final point. How does a community of friends who share the act of sharing respond to a member of the community who espouses racist comments, or perhaps is defined by a racist set of beliefs/racist identity? If the community loves whatever and is radically poor and improper, how can it respond to hateful or assaultive speech by its own members? Let's first speculate how the facilitator guided by tough love would respond. Perhaps she would say something like "[y]ou have the potential to be more than your racist ideas, and I am going to push you to change! You are better than this, smarter than this, and I am going to help you recover from racism." This version of love negates what a person is in the name of what they can and ought to become. For the love to be received, the student must trust in the teacher and believe the teacher's prognostication that the potential to change is present and will be verified in the future (as he or she might not be able to perceive this potentiality for him- or herself). The problem here is that confirmation rests in a future state that only the teacher can foresee. This hope for the future is equally accompanied by a cursing of the present as inadequate. Tough love thus bets on a certain level of trust (between student and teacher that may or may not be there to begin with) as well as hope (that indeed the future—as foreseen by the teacher—promises something that cannot be foreseen in the present). The love actually teacher would respond differently: "I love you just as you are! If you are a racist, I love you as a racist." This position might be more appalling than the previous as it rejects the possibility of change and resigns the student to his or her racist identity. Sadly, the racist identity would be blessed (accepted as destiny)! The implication is that the teacher herself might be a racist and finds a representation of her racist identity in the identity of the student (as a mirror reflection). But here is where whatever love can offer a third possibility. If a teacher loved whatever a student was, she might say, "I love that part of you that is not reducible to being a racist. I affirm that halo that surrounds you that is more than mere racism or your racist identity." Whereas the first two kinds of love have conditions—in the first, the condition is that you can and ought to no longer be a racist and the second is that you stay a racist—the third kind of love is radically unconditional in the sense that it affirms whatever one cannot not be (regardless of one's racist *identity*). It is love for the impotential, inessential supplement that is exposed through a person's identity, actions, or consciously held beliefs while at the same time escaping them. This is why whatever we are is, in a sense, outside of cursing or blessing—it is the comical (rather than tragic) supplement that is beyond good or evil. Whatever love, in this sense, is indifferent to the racist identity that tough love forces to change or that love actually clings to. And it is this indifference that makes all the difference as the student can no longer rebel against the curses or yearn for blessings. Instead, that which was seen as essential (the identity as this kind of person with these kinds of beliefs) become vestigial and unimportant while the inessential question of whatever one is in excess of the identity becomes essential!

The same holds true for friends in the community of infancy. Whatever love means that others in the community cannot (a) identify with such racist ideology (as something shared) and (b) can and should be critical of such beliefs and actions precisely because they unconditionally love whatever someone is. Being critical in this context does not mean cursing an identity (and thus returning to the authority of the Voice). Instead it means transforming a given identity into a question (and thus undermining any claims to identity as a necessary essence or destiny). This is especially true when it comes to forms of identity that have hardened into a specific ideology such as whiteness. Indeed, if identity concerns *having* (and therefore concerns the question of property), then whiteness is the epidemy of identity, especially in the United States.[36] As a corollary, views of minority students that reduce identity to a deficit or lack ought to be turned into a question, as the very notion of a "deficit" is itself predicated on a notion of the self as having (or in this case *not* having that which approximates whiteness as the only "legitimate" identity).[37] Remember, friends share the event of the outside rather than the inside (of identity as a property). As such, friendship *profanes* attempts to build community based on some kind of perceived sense of having (or in opposition to those who do not have). Instead, friends are infantile; they share a weak, impotential supplement that is almost nothing at all: the vibration at the edge of identity that displaces and suspends in yielding to a demand. And in this way, they can truly love one another without having to have.

Conclusion

In conclusion, what traditional and constructivist forms of love share is a sacrifice of whatever, of the potentiality of the student to not not-be, their manner of being. In the traditional model, potentiality is only valued as a means to another end (a future actualization) and in the constructivist classroom, potentiality falls out of the equation, leaving only what is, what has been actualized as an end in itself. What is missing is precisely that which defines whatever it is a student is as a pure means. To sacrifice whatever means that students are subjected to becoming an ideal that is predetermined by the natural order, world spirit, ontological vocations, or simply standardized efficiency protocols. Or students are subjected to the tyranny of what is, to the tyranny of the world as a necessary condition for selfhood to emerge as a form of having. To reclaim potentiality as a pure means (without relation to the question of ends) opens up a space and time where students might stumble upon their own potentiality to love. Hence the adventure of P4I!

5

Happiness

Like love, happiness is usually not the first thing that comes to mind when we think of education. In fact, for some of us it may be pretty far down the list. Insofar as we see a direct connection between happiness and education, happiness—not unlike the tough love variety of the love of the teacher ("You will thank me later!")—is seen as what education is meant to prepare us for, rather than what education is about. In other words, while we might agree that life—in its final instance—is about achieving happiness ("I just want my children to be happy!"), it is about the prospect of leading a happy life *in the future*. In fact, a lack of happiness (like a lack of genuine love) in our children's education may be considered a necessary evil/sacrifice to guarantee their future well-being (or, at least spare them future unhappiness). On the other hand, and maybe not surprisingly, there is an overriding emphasis in education on another—no less elusive—kind of sentiment: hope. Radical and reformist pedagogues call for hope. Critical and post-critical pedagogues insist on hope.[1] Indeed, some in educational philosophy even argue that we cannot conceive of education without some notion of hope.[2] But considering that hope could be defined as an anticipation of a happier life in the future, it is not only not surprising that hope (and not happiness) is given such a prominent place in theories of education, it could also be considered the most fitting (or paradigmatic) sentiment for a view of education as a preparation for a happier life to come. The same could be said about a conception of philosophy with children that aligns itself with this view of education by being directed at the realization of a more rational, more reasonable, and more just—in other words, a happier—world to come. The question is what it would mean to conceive of the community of inquiry (*qua* community of infancy) as a place and time where happiness can replace hope as a constitutive feature of education—rather than affirming this aspect of established educational forms of life. At stake here is, once again, a definition of educational life that is not predicated on negation or destiny but on sufficiency (a hopelessly happy form-of-educational-life).

The Role of Hope in Education

The idea of hope as an integral part of education is especially prevalent in critical and progressive theories of education. For Freire, for example, hope is a necessary feature of teaching because it implies that the teacher has a vision for where she wants to take the students (a vision for a better world that she wants the students to help realize). "Whatever the perspective through which we appreciate authentic educational practice," he writes, "its process implies hope. Unhopeful educators contradict their practice. They are men and women without address, and without a destination they are lost in history."[3] In addition, "[w]ithout a vision for tomorrow, hope is impossible."[4] In other words, without hope there is no vision (and vice versa), and without both/either there is no movement out of the present toward a better future. We find this emphasis on hope also in the work of Henry Giroux, who, in a recent article, refers to hope as "the desire for a future that offers more than the present."[5] And bell hooks, in *Teaching Community: A Pedagogy of Hope,* writes: "Educating is always a vocation rooted in hopefulness,"[6] and quoting the theologian Mary Grey: "Living in hope says to us, 'There is a way out,' even from the most dangerous and desperate situations."[7] In all cases, the message is the same: there would be nothing left except fatalism or cynicism in the present without hope and or the utopian imagination pointing a way out. So one of the ways in which hope is used is as sentiment, desire, or disposition (driving force) that allows educators and students alike to transcend the given and move toward (help realize) a better (more rational, just, equitable, democratic, etc.) world.

But there is, importantly, another—and in a certain way more prominent—sense in which hope is used in the work of some of these authors; a sense that de-emphasizes the future-oriented aspect of hope and sees it instead as directed to or perhaps at something that remains immanent to teaching and learning (the classroom community)—an experience of the very possibility of change, that is, a precondition for change as such. We find this in Freire, who refers to hope as the experience of the unfinishedness of the world, of its becoming. He writes: "The world is not finished. It is always in the process of becoming."[8] He also writes, "Hope is a natural, possible, and necessary impetus in the context of our unfinishedness. Hope is an indispensable seasoning in our human, historical experience."[9] In other words, the emphasis here is not on hope as directed toward a better world to come but on the very possibility of any kind of change, that things can be different. It is directed at something that is already here as a possibility in any communal educational practice and only needs to be allowed to manifest itself. "[H]ope," Freire writes, "is something shared between teachers and students. The hope that we can learn together, teach together, be curiously impatient together, produce something together, and resist together the obstacles that prevent the flowing of our joy."[10] In a similar vein, bell hooks speaks of hope as something that is present (or realizable) in the moment and directed not at the future so much as at what is possible in the moment:

> The academy is not Paradise. But learning is a place where paradise can be created. The classroom, with all its limitations, remains a location of possibility. In that field of possibility we have the opportunity to labor for freedom, to demand of ourselves and our comrades, an openness of mind and heart that allows us to face reality even as we collectively imagine ways to move beyond boundaries, to transgress. This is education as the practice of freedom.[11]

And in her more recent book *Teaching Community: A Pedagogy of Hope*, hooks specifically argues against education being (only) directed at the future and instead focuses on the need to be in the present, writing that "[c]ollege education is so often geared toward the future, the perceived rewards that the imagined future will bring that it is difficult to teach students that the present is a place of meaning."[12] Hope, on this view, turns us toward the present and a sense of community in the classroom, or perhaps realizing that there is a possibility that can be made manifest in the present that is somehow beyond the present. Rerouting hope from the future to the present and its potentiality is also found in the work of Naomi Hodgson, Joris Vlieghe, and Piotr Zamojski, whose post-critical manifesto equally affirms the world and the hope within and for that world.[13]

So we clearly have an emphasis on hope in education not as (primarily) directed at (a specific vision of) the future (preparing students for better lives to come), but as directed at the exposure or manifestation of an experience of a radical kind of openness to possibilities in the present that transgress or exceed or supersede existing limit conditions. But if this can really be said to be the dominant way of seeing the role of hope, at least in some of these theoretical accounts (i.e., being about attuning us to what is present yet neglected in the world as it is), hope is really about our present educational practice as a place and time of possibilities (what is possible in the moment/the current situation in the classroom, as it is). It is not the hope for something else to become possible in the future (happiness in deferral), but for something possible to happen with what is within and against the contemporary moment. In other words, it is about making the classroom a place and time where, as hooks put it, "paradise can be created," right now through the slightest of shifts, through the smallest of gestures. What we want to emphasize is that for these authors, there is an ontological claim to be made here even if it is never stated clearly. Whereas the common sense notion of hope presupposes that potentiality comes first and that it is then actualized in the future (hence the future-oriented notion of hope and the utopian imagination), we might be able to read some of the citations provided above as *inverting the order* between potentiality and actuality. It would seem that the realization of potentiality *comes about after or through* education, not as a presupposition that must wait to be actualized in a future to come, but as a moment of happiness in the present. But in that case, hope is no longer used in a commonsense way, and, in fact, we could say that it is exactly about abandoning hope understood in everyday language that makes this kind of experience possible (by turning our gaze to the present), turning the sentiment from one of hope for (*qua* anticipation of) happiness in the future, to one of the manifestation of happiness in the educational present (realization of something that is already there, namely the potential for human freedom and happiness). There is no other choice than to face the present, to see what can be done—one of those things being to engage in studious play (or put language to use and babble!) without the need to hope for something better at a future point to come. It is in this sense that we could say that it may be more appropriate to ask for a hopelessly happy kind of pedagogical practice (in which hope is replaced by happiness as the dominant sentiment).

P4I as a Hopelessly Happy Pedagogical Practice (toward a Pedagogy of Hopelessness)

We can perhaps turn back to P4C to provide an alternative to the emphasis on hope (or rather, the future-oriented variety of hope, in education), again using one of the founding P4C theorists, Sharp, as our point of departure. Indeed, Sharp argues that happiness is an essential feature of doing philosophy with children. Instead of more or less instrumental reasons for pursing philosophical inquiry in schools (such as making better judgments, or cultivating wisdom, or improving school learning outputs), Sharp highlights happiness as a more basic motivating factor. More importantly, Sharp argues that happiness is not a state attached to the achievement of ends or of accomplishment or even well-being. Instead, happiness is a kind of "disposition" that "is not something that can be sought and thereby achieved directly."[14] Likewise, it cannot be given to us by another. Happiness arises from inside the inquiry process itself in such a way as to put emphasis on "*being* rather than *having*."[15] Here, Sharp seems to suggest that happiness is attached to our being-thus (or whatever being) as Agamben would say. In fact, Sharp provocatively states that happiness is when a child "stands in awe of the possibilities of human nature."[16] Note that it is not potentiality *for x* that produces happiness; it is rather the awe of potentiality *as such* in our thusness, which produces happiness for Sharp. This is not a notion of happiness predicated on *having* so much as happiness predicated on exposure to potentiality, or perhaps more directly, exposure to infancy (a state of non-having within having that gives having away and thus opts for use). It is, to recall our analysis of monastic rules in Chapter 2, a state of radical *poverty* (of not having). This is a shocking ending to an essay in which Sharp argues repeatedly for a concept of self and action that is necessarily founded on a "developmental teleology" oriented toward "purposes or plans in which genuinely novel directions can and do emerge."[17] Speech is oriented toward fulfilling a certain teleological directionality. The P4C facilitator guides such speech toward reasonableness as the "ultimate criterion"[18] for judging the efficacy of P4C. And then, at the end of this teleologically directed argument comes a non-teleological moment of suspension in the form of happiness. Happiness is the awe in experiencing potentiality within speech without it having to be directed at anything beyond itself. It is the being of speech rather than the having of skills that emerges as foundational to the P4C experience. In this sense, Sharp turns back to potentiality (and thus also impotentiality) in the very moment when P4C appears to be at its teleological end. It is almost as if awe at potentiality (rather than what has been accomplished in terms of the skills one has) is discovered through the course of dialogue, and that it is only when potentiality proceeds (rather than precedes) the actualization of skills that happiness is truly possible. Happiness is precisely what emerges when this end is left idle within the community, and it is exposed to its potentiality (infancy) for speech (de-completing any teleological end with awe). Moreover, individual happiness, for Sharp, is intimately tied to the happiness of the other members of the community. In "What Is a 'Community of Inquiry'?" she writes that one of the aims of the practice of P4C is to form communities that engender "a care for one another's happiness equal to the concern one has for one's own happiness."[19] What makes these formulations significant is that the emphasis is not on the future, but on the fact that the practice "engenders" happiness in the course of the practice, that is, that it realizes a sense of communal well-being as the essence of the practice. In other words, like the bonds of love that form between its members, happiness is made possible by the way in which the members of the community relate to each other as radically open/beings of potentiality, as friends, as whatever they are without identity.

Rather than just another facet of the P4C experience, we want to take the disruptive nature of Sharp's conclusion seriously and argue that this shift toward happiness opens the way for P4I to emerge. In this sense, Sharp's comments on happiness are not actually an end to her essay but rather a messianic opening to infancy: an infancy that is no longer instrumentalized, without destiny (direction/telos), and without end. Agamben can help us extend Sharp's theory of happiness, and in this sense help us postpone the ending of her essay even further until the very notion of an end ceases to be relevant.

Agamben on Happiness as (a Practice in) Hopelessness

Agamben's project, in its entirely, could perhaps be summarized as an exploration of the concept form-of-life. What does it mean to contemplate a life that is inseparable from its form? Or, stated differently, what does it mean to contemplate a life that lacks any negation (separation or division between *phone* and *logos*, human and animal, potentiality and actuality) and any destination (is without *telos*, vocation, or necessary ends)? This would be a life that lives only its livability or its potentiality without this potentiality being sacrificed or predetermined in any way. The problem with capitalism is precisely that life's potentiality (its labor power) is expropriated and thus divided against its form. The result—at least in the classical Marxist model—is some kind of alienation, or a radical reduction of what is livable in a life to one's position within a division of labor. Yet for Agamben, such negation and destiny can be overcome through a form-of-life. A form-of-life would be whatever life it is, or a life lived thusly, full of its potentiality for this *and* that without division. "[O]nly that life is happy," he writes, "in which the division disappears."[20] Form-of-life is happy because there is no longer a division separate life from its form, actuality from its potentiality. And: "That is why human beings—as beings of power who can do or not do, succeed or fail, lose themselves or find themselves—are the only beings for whom happiness is always at stake in their living, the only beings whose life is irremediably and painfully assigned to happiness."[21] Claiming our impotentiality (rather than sacrificing it in the passage from animal to human, child to adult, potentiality to actualization) is what "irremediable and painfully" consigns us to happiness. We are consigned to happiness and this is always what is at stake in our living. But what is happiness?

For Aristotle, happiness was a necessary human *telos* or an absolute end for which all else is done. It was, in Aristotle's philosophy, an end in itself, or a pure end orienting the good life. It was the goal of ethics to promote happiness or flourishing through the habituation of the virtues via proper education. In the fulfilled life, a person would act in the right ways, at the right times, toward the right things/people, for the right purposes. This is a life of *praxis* that is informed by correct feeling and thinking oriented by an understanding of the ultimate good (happiness or flourishing). Opposed to Aristotle, Agamben turns toward Plato. In Plato's later works, Agamben finds a way to think human life that neutralizes the means-end relationship that dominates Aristotle's thinking. According to Agamben's reading, Plato posits a new notion of happiness that is not conceived of as an end guiding action. Instead, happiness is immanent to contemplation as a regressive movement (*katabaino*) that discovers the potentiality for thought's thinkability (or speaking's speakability). In contemplative forms-of-life, happiness is immanent to life as such, without dividing life into means and ends. What makes such immanence happy? Agamben posits that "life is what is produced in the very act of its exercise as delight internal to the act, as if by dint of gesticulating the hand in the end found its pleasure in its 'use'; the eye by constantly looking became enamored with vision; the legs, by bending rhythmically, invented walking."[22] In other words, happiness comes from use (rather than functionality). By simply doing whatever the limbs and organs are doing, they become "enamored" and thus find a use in and through their gesticulations. These gesticulations do not have an internal telos guiding them toward a predetermined end point (in terms of the fulfilled life of virtue). Instead, they merely experiment with whatever they can do (with their potentiality to be thus) and this experimentation produces a form-of-life that is of use (to itself). Stated differently, the organs and limbs Agamben describes do not have an identity. Instead, they are movements, ticks, gesticulations that seem to escape any purpose, and yet they invent particular modes of life through play that is sufficient in itself. Happiness is, simply put, "absolutely profane 'sufficient life' that has reached the perfection of its own power and its own communicability."[23] This is a life that does not sacrifice its impotentiality but rather finds within it new uses that are not predetermined according to an essence or telos. Happy life is a life that uses itself to generate itself; it is a life that has not fulfilled its telos so much as a life that is a pure means without end determining what it should or should not do, should or should not be in advance of its singular becoming.

This kind of sufficiency is not to be read as mere acceptance of the way things are or of the status quo. In fact, the status quo absolutely rejects living thusly. The whole impetus driving the learning society is that the subject is never sufficient, must constantly be learning in order to improve outputs and performances, or to remain flexible for the gig economy. To prefer not to partake in constant learning is to put one's self at risk of being abandoned by the learning society. Living thusly means embracing the way things are *without identity and without functionality.* Agamben summarizes, "[E]verything here, in fact, stay[s] the same, but loses its identity."[24] In this sense, we are "irremediably and painfully assigned to happiness" not as an end point but as a condition of possibility within the lives that we live that is not exhausted or used up in the identities we perform or the function assigned to our gestures. It would be a life that suspends and renders inoperative *what we have learned* to be, do, and say in order to open up a sphere of play (instead of *praxis*). Notice that for Agamben there is no mention of hope at this point. Happiness is not something we *hope* to achieve in the future through a specific kind of learning. Instead, it is present in the life that we are living as a continual potentiality: Not as a potentiality *to come* but rather as potentiality as such (the ability to speak/not to speak that we return to in every speaking act).

Pushing this point further, we could also argue that not only is the learning society fueled by a future-oriented hope for a better tomorrow. In addition, this hope is always also a *curse* against the affirmation of the present, which must be negated in order to reach some kind of deferred fulfillment. In this case, the hope that has been absorbed into the learning society comes at a cost: *guilt* over what has not yet been achieved, a sense of failure to live up to the command to actualize a potentiality for a greater purpose (be that liberation, democracy, or revolution). In this sense, we find ourselves yet again caught in a vicious cycle wherein negation and destiny intervene to separate being from its potentiality in the present as a condition of happiness. Whereas many of the theorist cited above simply affirm hope without recognizing its complicity with the learning society, we would like to offer a more positive foundation for education, one that is not predicated on either negation or destiny but on the happiness of infancy as such.

Infancy is an experience of the potentiality to speak within speech that produces its own kind of happiness—happiness in the playful use of speech that is undestined for any function and deposes any law of learning that would assign (ahead of time) assessment values to this or that kind of speech. Recall that for Agamben, what characterizes humans is that "there is no essence, no historical or spiritual vocation, no biological destiny that humans must enact or realize,"[25] and that the only thing humans have to be, consists in *"the simple fact of one's existence as possibility or potentiality."*[26] More specifically, we have language, and language allows us to articulate how we think of ourselves, but how we use language is not pre-determined, which, in turn, means a radical openness to new uses. For Agamben, realizing more fully this defining feature of our being is a source of happiness. He writes: "The impropriety, which we expose as our proper being, manner, which we *use*, engenders us. It is our second, happier, nature."[27] Notice that happiness is not nature. It is not a *necessary* necessity of our essence as human beings (a special telos that defines humans in a certain way). But rather, happiness is a *second* nature or a *contingent* necessity found in our manner of being. Remember from Chapter 4 that manner is that which one cannot not be or do. It is what we yield to, and in yielding to it, we become happy. Because we cannot not help but express our manners, they are necessary, but they are also radically contingent at the same time. There is nothing predetermined about manners, which are emergent, and through their emergence, they engender whatever we are (in some unquantifiable, idiosyncratic way). Manners are the spin, or halo that surrounds our *habitus*, making us singularly in a way that interrupts any attempt to assign an identity or measure to our being-thusly. But why is this second nature considered happy? What is it about manners that opens the human up to happiness? Manners are not actions that can be evaluated. They are not virtues that are guaranteed to cultivate happiness because they are anchored in a human telos. Instead, they are happy because they are precisely beyond judgment and thus have been blissfully abandoned as inessential supplements that, precisely because of this seemingly vestigial status, are the key to happiness. Manners play with themselves, use themselves, and do so in relation to the demand of existence that comes from within life itself. Happiness, on this reading, is not added to life but is always already there in how life uses itself to create a form-of-life.

Agamben himself offers testimony to the peculiar happiness of contemplation and study. When asked whether he thought the image others had of him was that of being a "thinker whose wisdom has come at the cost of ease, affection, joy, the animal pleasures," Agamben responded: "These images are made to protect people from the risks that come with thinking about things. The opposite is of course the case. The relation of reflection to sensation, joy, and pleasure is that it sharpens and extends each one."[28] In this seemingly passing comment, we find an important point about studying (in the broad sense of study that describes Agamben's life), namely that, for him it is something that is inherently pleasurable, something that affirms happiness, in the sense of both intensifying the "animal pleasures" and "sharpening" them through an increase in consciousness and intellectual awareness (thus cultivating a second nature or form-of-life that is a composite of manners). Happiness is not essential. Rather it is the inessential halo that surrounds the manner of our study (an event, a vibration in our being), which is so subtle that it is easily missed by those who are not themselves studiers.

Just like we may have experienced this kind of studying as happy (in the way articulated above), we can propose that the educational use of study should be seen as allowing students to experience (the possibility) of a particular form of a happy life, a life that lacks the need to actualize anything in particular in a measurable and thus quantifiable sense. But what characterizes this educational life without end is that it is not some form of meditation (in the sense of a ceasing of striving or movement, selflessness, nonaction, which we find in Stoicism or Taoism). Rather it is an activity that entails a momentum toward something, only that that something remains immanent to the process of studying: its own, immanent use of itself that is demanded of itself. This happiness is not the happiness found in the learning society, which appears to be perpetually deferred for a future when we have passed the test, or graduated, or paid off our student loans. These are driven by certain hopes (even if the hopes are rather banal) and thus always have a sense of delay and anticipation that accompanies them. There is a sense of being indebted to a future, of investing in a vision that is to come that fuels the hopes underlying the learning society. But the happiness of studious play—especially in a community of infancy—is not simply opposite of leaning either and instead is about a certain kind of rhythm that only emerges when the ends of learning are suspended and the means are experienced as such (language and speakability, for instance).

While the focus above has been on the individual experience of studying as a source of happiness (and it should be pointed out that happiness is of course always experienced by an individual), we can distinguish between the kind of ease that is made possible by the experience of infancy when we study alone, and the kind of ease that becomes possible only when we engage in a communal experience of infancy with others. As we have seen through our analysis of infancy and communal study, the community that becomes possible is one of love and friendship (see Chapter 4). Now, we may think of those terms themselves as inherently desirable, and almost as synonyms for happiness. And especially with regard to friendship, where Aristotle speaks of experiencing "sweetness of being," this is certainly the case. So one of the ways in which communal study may allow for an experience of happiness is the kind of desubjectification that happens when we see others as other selves (*heteros autos*), leading to an experience of *ek-stasis* (standing outside of oneself), an expansion of self beyond one's facticity, and a communion with others. Rules are the form that this collective form-of-life takes up through the use of itself. Thus rules make for happy life only insofar as they depose any law held over collective life (such as the laws of learning or the laws of reasonableness).

We want to come back here to what has already been said about the idea of form-of-life and why we should think of a community that embraces infancy as a happier community, and the realization of such a community in education, as a paradigm for such a community. For Agamben, the nature of the in-tentional community is exemplified in the Franciscan Monastic Order. While not a specifically educational form-of-life, the monastic order is comparable to the educational community in P4I, in that life in the latter could be said to not be distinguishable from its form. About such a life, Agamben writes:

> A life that cannot be separated from its form is a life for which what is at stake in its way of living is living itself. What does this formulation mean? It defines a life—human life—in which the single ways, acts, and processes of living are never simply *facts* but always and above all *possibilities* of life, always and above all power. Each behavior and each form of human living is never prescribed by a specific biological vocation, nor is it assigned by whatever necessity; instead, no matter how customary, repeated, and socially compulsory, it always puts at stake living itself. That is why human beings—as beings of power who can do or not do, succeed or fail, lose themselves or find themselves—are the only beings for whom happiness is always at stake in their living, the only beings whose life is irremediably and painfully assigned to happiness.[29]

It is in this sense that Agamben writes that "[a] political life" is "a life directed toward the idea of happiness."[30] And, again, as we have already seen in the previous section, where we described the life of the studier as a "sufficient life," the in-tentional community of the P4I classroom could be described as a communal educational life "[t]hat has reached the perfection of its own power of its own communicability."[31] To be more specific, an education in and for infancy is an education that finds happiness in the use of language—in speaking speaking's speakability, returning speech to its potentiality to be spoken. An infantile education is thus an education that untethers speaking from any identity (as proper or improper, reasonable or unreasonable) and any destiny (within a democratic society).

At this point, it is important to turn toward a possible critique of this kind of happiness. Some might argue that abandoning hope in the name of happiness is a kind of resignation. On this interpretation, hope is what drives educators, especially those who are teaching underserved populations. This is certainly a real-world problem that needs to be addressed by anyone proposing a critique of hope. In response, we would simply say that phenomenologically speaking, the facilitator of P4I is not driven by hopes. Rather, he/she is driven by the love of students and happiness to be in the classroom. In our personal experience, hope is not a motivating factor when in the community of infancy. Instead, one is deeply engrossed in what is happening and taking pleasure in that happening. Without such happiness, it would be hard to imagine how the facilitator would continue on without burning out. Indeed, it is not at all clear how hope can stave off burn out when happiness is somehow continually deferred to the future. Those who insist on hope have perhaps invested too much *faith* in hope and its "transformative" powers. Yet instead of an orientation that says "I am burned out and will have to struggle to gain happiness tomorrow," we would argue that saying "I am happy and will struggle to protect what I am doing" is the strongest kind of motivator. While the former waits for happiness to arrive (or laments its passing), the latter is radically *impatient* and *active* in exploring happiness in the present and how to develop ease with students through the use of language that is demanded by language's infancy. Another way of stating this is that one is predicated on a negation while the other is predicated on an affirmation. And this does not mean that everything is perfect; rather it means that teachers and students feel that there is a practice—P4I for instance—through which an educational form-of-life has emerged that is sufficient, that is whatever it is, and that in its being-thus is happy. Such a happy life does not merely abide by normal operating conditions, rather it suspends them *right now*, in the name of an educational adventure, even if there are institutional risks to such a (profane) gesture.

The Comedy of Happiness

The critical teacher who is driven by hope is deadly serious. He or she thinks of teaching as a political action (a *praxis*), an intervention into the present in the name of actualizing a future potentiality. This is tough love in the name of human emancipation to come. This is hope for a better tomorrow through education as cultivation for a democratic future. And there is a certain amount of guilt that comes with "failing" to live up to this image of what could be achieved in the future. Here, we do not want to discount this project or undervalue its importance in transformative projects. Instead, we want to merely suggest that there might be another way of thinking about teaching that does not fall nicely into categories of either conservative or leftist in any traditional sense, and in doing so replaces the conceptual framework for thinking about education from tough love to whatever love and from hope to hopeless happiness. This would likewise mean a shift from thinking about the gestures of the teacher as embodying a *serious action*. Here, we define action as that which is imputable to a subject who, in turn, is responsible for acting. Hence the *seriousness* of acting—there are consequences that one has to bear. The serious teacher views teaching as an action, the consequences of which are born out in the performance of his or her students. Teaching as a serious action is exceptionally ingrained in our way of thinking about educational relationships. Authors as diverse as Paulo Freire to Gert Biesta describe teaching as a *praxis*.[32] How can teaching be anything but a serious action? Opposed to this tried and true logic, we would like to end this chapter by arguing that in P4I, the facilitator is disruptive precisely because of his or her *comedic* suspension of action in the name of infantile speech. In the end, it is precisely the comedic dimension of education unleashed through P4I that opens the possibility for happiness in the classroom to appear. As Agamben writes, "Comedy defines ... a sphere of human life in which happiness is not determined by action and from which, for that reason, all suffering is excluded."[33] We are interested in exploring the ramifications for this assertion in relation to P4I.

In the book *Karman: A Brief Treatise on Action, Guilt, and Gesture*, Agamben pinpoints a particular problem that humanity has yet to come to terms with: the mystery of imputation or how we become responsible for our actions. The knot tying subject to his or her actions is the threshold across which a subject is constituted as *subjected* to the law (as culpable and therefore punishable). In his work, Agamben attempts to suspend the operations of the complex juridical apparatus found in Western culture that increasingly ties actor to action in such a way that the actor internalizes fault. Summarizing his hypothesis, Agamben writes, "[T]he concept of *crimen*, of action that is sanctioned, which is to say, imputable and productive of consequences, stands at the foundation not only of law, but also of the ethics and religious morality of the West."[34] A turning point in the complex story of ethics and religious morality in the West pre-dates Christianity. Somewhat counterintuitively, Agamben locates a key origin point in Greek tragedy, which situates the question of freedom and guilt in the precarious gap that separates and unites agency (to be the cause of one's actions) and divine fate (to be acted upon) in the actions of the hero. Unlike traditional readings of Greek tragedy, Agamben does not locate the dilemma between the internal feeling of the actor to be the free cause of his or her actions and the whims of the Gods so much as *within* the privileging of action as such. Once action has been connected to actor, the question of imputation and the assignment of guilt become the inevitable "criterion of ethics and of humanity."[35] The result is that the history of the West plays out in the shadow of tragedy, as actors are now always divided between innocence and guilt.

The second upshot of the tragic emphasis on action is that humanity is perpetually separated from its happiness. Agamben writes,

> From the perspective that interests us here, what is decisive is thus that praxis, human action, appears as the dimension that is opened up for the sake of the good, as what must actualize the final end toward which human beings cannot but aim. This means that between human beings and their good there is not a coincidence, but a fracture and a gap, which action … seeks incessantly to fill.[36]

Notice that action (a) has a function that must (b) negate the present in the name of (c) that which humans must necessarily aim at (as their destiny). Humans find themselves *in debt* to their own end, and action is the sphere where this debt is continually reasserted. One must act in such and such a way so as to achieve the destined happiness. Yet because of the gap that action attempts to overcome, the promised happiness can only be hoped for. What humanity is left with is an infinite deferral of an end to come and the fault that they must bear in the meantime as evidence of their tragic failure. The result is similar to the split inaugurated within language by the apparatus of the oath that continually blesses life just as much as it curses it (discussed in Chapter 1).

And this is no different with the history of educational philosophy. A host of educational philosophers locate teaching squarely within the framework of tragedy.[37] Teaching is tragic because the teacher finds him- or herself in and through actions and their risky consequences. Or, from another perspective, the teacher assumes the mysteries of education through tragic actions.[38] Teaching, on this account, is doomed to the inevitability of loss, disappointment, and doubt. Indeed, much like the tragic model identified by Agamben, the tragedy of teaching is derived from the inherent antinomy that exists between the autonomy of the teacher (as actor) and as professional (acted upon by the institution) now internalized through a sense of inevitable failure. The teacher bears responsibility for these antinomies through his or her actions.

But is this the only way to conceptualize teaching? Here we can perhaps pivot to philosophy for children. For Agamben, there is another paradigm at work in Western culture—one that does not privilege acting but rather thinking. If the former is best represented by Aristotle then the latter is best represented by Socrates. Within this second paradigm, ethics shifts from the connection between actor and action (and in turn, responsibility and fault) to contemplation. Socrates, on this reading, emerges as an anti-tragic figure who seeks truth not through action but through thought. Indeed, Socrates is critiqued precisely because of his lack of action, lack of profession, and lack of income. He is without works and deeds, but for this reason is, on all accounts, all the happier. Another way of putting this is that Socrates (and by extension, philosophy) privileges potentiality over actuality, privileging means over ends. For us, this suggests that P4C might be a way to return teaching to an ethic beyond the tragic, and in this sense, reclaim a little bit of happiness in education. But in the classical model of P4C, this dimension of thinking is foreclosed upon when thought is instrumentalized and absorbed into a means-end framework that promotes the development of a certain set of skills in order to fulfill a certain telos. Lost here is the adventure of thinking when it is opened up to exploring its own potentiality without negation or destiny. This is precisely why P4I is needed: to reconnect thinking back to an anti-tragic (happy) paradigm.

But for Agamben, the idea is not so much to simply affirm contemplation (and potentiality) *over* and *above* action (and actualization). Instead, it is to look for forms-of-life that are defined by impotential actions, or actions that deactivate themselves: contemplative forms-of-life. Such actions would not be the product of an action forcing potentiality to actualize itself (and thus sacrifice impotentiality) so much as the result of a yielding or allowing of impotentiality to materialize. Is there some kind of action that is unjudgeable, meaning an action that neutralizes the nexus that connects actor, action, and responsibility? How can we imagine such a thing? Is there, in other words, an action that decompletes itself and thus is happy (rather than guilty)? For Agamben, *comedy* offers another possibility for conceptualizing the relationship between subject and action, one that sidesteps the issue of the internalization of fault. Unlike tragedy, comedy presents us with characters *without action*. Theatrical personas imitate characters (not actions), and in this way, are ethically not imputable. Think of the slapstick antics of toons or comedic mimes. Their gestures are wild and disruptive, but we do not fault them as they are not "actions" in any traditional sense. Instead of judging the "actions," we laugh at them in their innocent exuberance. Having suspended actions, the subject is removed from the burden of being responsible and attending judgments that assign fault. Charlie Chaplin might very well destroy the entirety of the factory, yet the audience cannot judge his gestures precisely because they are not actions. A comedic actor like Chaplin does not will actions that express character but rather exposes his characteristic manners as such, and in this sense, cannot be cursed or blessed. Manners are not actions manifesting the strength and virtue of an actor but rather are manifestations of impotentiality or a weakness in an agent's being. And in this way, the equation wedding together means (actions) and ends (happiness) via action is neutralized.

Interestingly, Agamben cites Aquinas as an inspiration. Aquinas writes, "Of course, there are some actions that do not seem to be carried out for the sake of an end. Examples are playful and contemplative actions, and those that are done without attention, like rubbing one's beard and the like. These examples could make a person think that there are some cases of acting without end."[39] In other words, acts of play, of contemplation, and of involuntary gestures (manners) all seem to suggest a form-of-life that cannot be judged according to the merits of its motivations or the virtues (or vices) of its actions. Instead, what is offered is a mode of being that is *sufficiently happy* as an open-ended means, continually experimenting with the parameters of what qualifies as a life. There is no purpose orienting actions and no will *forcing* potentiality to actualize itself. Instead, there is a sense of allowing one's being to be thusly, or whatever it is. Another way of saying this is that playing, studying, and our manners all are forms of use, where functionality (always oriented toward an end) is left idle. Indeed, isn't this precisely what the comedic persona "teaches"—that the world can be deactivated, suspended, and thus open for studious play? Here, happiness is not invested in an end to come so much as it is lived as a means (without judgment and without end). In sum, P4I returns P4C to its promised happiness by enhancing its comical potentiality. And in turn, P4I offers Agamben a practice that does not simply privilege potentiality over actuality but rather opens up education to a sphere of inoperative speech acts where students practice speaking infancy (through comedic babble).

This returns us to the discussion of adventure offered in Chapter 3. We would argue that the adventurer is not the hero. The figure of the hero belongs to the tragic theater. They are the serious individuals whose actions determine their character. Instead, we want to suggest that the real star of the adventure is perhaps none other than the comedian, or, in Agamben's work, Pulcinella. Characterizing the trickster figure of Pulcinella, Agamben writes:

> *Despite the stereotypical pretense of a plot, in the comedy of Pulcinella there is only parabasis. Pulcinella does not act in a play; he has always already interrupted it, has always already left it, by means of a shortcut or a byway. He is pure parabasis: an*

exit from the scene, from history, from the silly, flimsy story in which one would like to contain him. In the life of humans—and this is his teaching—the only important thing is to find an escape route. Leading where? To the origin.[40]

Pulcinella does not act but rather interrupts action. And this is his teaching: that there is an exit from the actor-action-imputation apparatus defining Western society. Pulcinella teaches by making the audience laugh at his actions, which are deactivated in the very act that activates them, revealing the pure mediality of his mannerisms and of his strange speaking. When the skillful is allowed to become clumsy, when the trembling of mannerisms overtake the proper functioning of actions and linguistic utterances, then the body and language are equally opened up for possible use. Nothing is negated or destroyed here. At the same time, nothing fulfills its destiny. Instead, all that remains are gesticulating babbling bodies whose happiness is found in free use.

In relation to education, we suggest that an emphasis on comedy releases the burden of the teacher from having to take serious action fueled by hope. These narratives are tragic, even when they achieve great things. We also suggest releasing the figure of the teacher from being a hero whose job it is to save others. Instead, we offer a rather weak and strange image of the teacher-as-not-a-teacher: the P4I facilitator as a clown, and the P4I session as a kind of comedic theater, or (improvised) clowning routine, wherein ends are suspended for experiment with the speech and its speakability that emerge. The coming community of infancy is a comedic community that is subversive in so far as it suspends the laws of learning not because of love for the future so much as love for whatever appears in the present through use. Like Pulcinella, the P4I facilitator creates an *exit* in the classroom—an exit from predetermined ways of speaking and thinking. This is serious! But only insofar as it is hilariously happy. And like all great clowns, the facilitator effaces his or her will (to dominate, to be in control, to embody the Voice of authority). Instead, the facilitator keeps babbling, uncontrollably.

We can circle back here to what has been said about the P4I facilitator as teacher-as-not-a-teacher and his or her role of using his or her power to uphold the laws of the schoolhouse, while also suspending the substantive part of the oath (sacrament of language) to make space for the demand of the potential of language (i.e., its infancy) to be exposed. Describing the teacher in the P4I classroom as a clown may help clarify the ambiguous role of the teacher as teacher-as-not-a-teacher (i.e., as both representative/part of an institution, which provides him or her with power, and, at the same time, being the one who subverts/undermines the law of learning). Like the clown, the teacher "occupies an ambiguous position between political inclusion and exclusion, between inside and outside."[41] As with other liminal figures in Agamben's work, the teacher-as-not-a-teacher is neither fully inside nor outside. On the one hand, he or she embodies the law of the schoolhouse (maintaining the classroom, for instance). On the other hand, he or she suspends and renders inoperative the law of learning that the schoolhouse serves (by opening up a space and time for the free use of language in response to the demand of infancy). This is also why the teacher-as-not-a-teacher is a strange kind of sovereign power that is always already at risk of sacrificing him- or herself, as the law of the schoolhouse might very well deem clowning as "unprofessional" behavior for a teacher. Thus the clown is a highly precarious role to play, yet a role that is absolutely necessary for the kind of happiness that philosophical contemplation can offer to participants in a P4I session.

While this might seem rather outrageous, Agamben himself argues that comedy and philosophy are tightly connected. Indeed, his project is precisely to show that "comedy is more ancient and profound than tragedy—something upon which many already agree—but also that it is closer to philosophy, so close that the two ultimately seem to blur into each other."[42] This is precisely because both comedy and contemplation concern pure means (instead of means to an end), purposiveness without a purpose, love for whatever rather than love for identity, and the flowering of mannerisms over and above the determinacy of style.

Conclusion

P4I as a reconceptualization of P4C repotentializes what is already present in P4C, and in the idea of the community of inquiry in particular, namely that it is ultimately about an experience, a being-thus in the present—a being-thus that happens/is being realized in the now, but only in the weakly utopian sense of realizing the experience of possibility (through the adventure of exploring ways of being without the guarantee offered by a human nature or essence). Experiencing and maintaining this experience is what constitutes an educational life as a form-of-life (as that which constitutes itself through its manner of being). This also means that it can do without hope, as there is nothing in particular to hope for, which replaces the questionable pleasure of anticipating happier times to come with the realization of the possibility of happiness in the present. Instead of being directed at the future, our gaze can turn toward each other, embracing/fully aware of the bonds of love and friendship that connect us (as we experience ourselves and others as potential beings), realizing that things are right (sufficient) as they are because we use what we need (having language) to begin (if we choose) the greatest adventure of all: speaking to each other, sharing our experience in a never-ending conversation, blissfully unaware of deadlines, finding a wayfaring purposiveness in babbling. Such is the comedy of studious play with friends.

6

Anarchy

Thus far, each chapter has employed the concept of contact: contact between participants and language, students and facilitator, rules and communities, and individuals in that community and each other. We have intentionally avoided the word "relationship." While the term "relationship" is popular in educational philosophy—indeed there is even an edited volume titled *No Education without Relation*[1]—we would offer up the suggestion that relation is not reducible to contact as experienced in P4I. According to Agamben, relationship as an ontological category is problematic as it always emerges from the presupposition of at least two different identities that must be put into relation. In learning relations, these identities are often formulated according to the immature and the mature, the ignorant and the knowledgeable, the adult and the child, and so forth. We can develop this idea further and suggest that all relations concern means and ends. For instance, learners view teachers as a means to achieving certain ends in the form of skill development or graduation certificates. And perhaps teachers view students as a means to achieving their ends (as professionals whose salary depends on learning outcomes). Yet for Agamben, there is a paradoxical space and time that suspends relationality. This is a contact point, or point of neutralization that puts into play free use through the sudden appearance of potentiality. This is why Agamben can argue that potentiality "is capable of always deposing ontological-political relations in order to cause a contact … to appear between their elements [manners, gestures that cannot be assigned specific identities and specific values within a law]."[2] It thus concerns "intimacy," which Agmaben describes as a space "unmediated by any articulation or representation."[3]

    It is our wager that P4I concerns contact rather than relation. There emerges an educational contact within the space and time of contemplation that suspends preconstituted identities and necessary teleologies (hence the idea of the teacher-as-not-a-teacher as well as an undestined notion of infancy). This is not, as stated throughout this book, a negation. It is merely a deactivation of the activity of relations (and the need to always *build* something to suture over the gap between constituted identities). This contact touches that which is presupposed by relationality but never thematized: potentiality (to do and not to do something, to be and not to be someone). Perhaps we can go so far as to say that if there is no education without relation, then *there is no studious play without contact*. This contact happens when the law of learning is suspended and the student and facilitator (teacher-as-not-a-teacher) start to babble without predefined destinations in mind. In this scenario, the role of the facilitator is not to cause or verify learning so much as to keep open a space and time for the studious play with language that, in a certain way, preexists relationality as a common form of infancy that both the facilitator and students share (although they share it in different, asymmetrical ways).

We will end this book with one final point of contact between P4I and politics. There seem to be two paradigms for thinking about politics and education. First, there is the instrumental approach that reduces education to a means to an externally defined political end. Liberal educational theory is symptomatic of this (i.e., education as preparation for democratic life). We can think here of P4C and how it is often cast as preparation for democratic citizenship. Sharp summarizes this telos nicely with the following opening to the essay aptly titled "The Community of Inquiry: Education for Democracy": "I would like to focus on the classroom community of inquiry as an educational means of furthering the sense of community that is a precondition for actively participating in a democratic society. The community of inquiry cultivates skills of dialogue, questioning, reflective inquiry and good judgement"[4] that are essential features of a global democratic society. Likewise, Lipman writes, "One might say, to employ a metaphor of instrumentalism, that the lathe on which the democracy-to-be is turned is equipped with a great many cutting tools, of which at least three are facets of the discipline of philosophy,"[5] including the open-ended ideas of truth, justice, and freedom; the centrality of higher-order thinking processes; and an emphasis on dialogue and deliberation when making judgments, all of which are cornerstones of P4C. Sharp and Lipman both emphasize how adult, democratic citizenship calls for a philosophical education at a young age. In this sense, philosophy is an instrument of democracy, and perhaps its most important instrument.

While the intentions are noble, the worry with this paradigm is that education will lose its *educational* value and become nothing more than a means for creating a particular end (a certain notion of a political community). This instrumentalization predetermines what counts as reasonableness and directs such reasonableness toward a destiny (a political telos). Of course, there is the noninstrumental approach that asserts the autonomy of education (and philosophy, for that matter) from politics. We can find this perspective in a number of conservative educational camps that assert various arguments for education as an end in itself. While addressing the issue of instrumentalization, in fully separating education from politics, it nevertheless produces another problem: the charge of elitism and/or quietism in the face of political, social, and economic inequalities. Education becomes detached from the problems of political life. Using Agamben as a point of departure, we suggest a rethinking of education (and P4I more specifically) as a pure means. To make this argument, we put forward the following theses. First, P4I is, at its base, an occupation of educational infrastructure (language, the classroom, desks, equipment, etc.) that suspends the function of this infrastructure within an administered learning society. Second, such activity becomes political when the occupation of infrastructure is made into a public issue. Third, the politics that arises from this occupation is troubling and disconcerting because it is a noninstrumental politics that cannot be reduced to a set of clearly defined goals or objectives. The same process can happen in reverse. One can start with a public occupation of infrastructure, and the non-teleological nature of such occupation lends itself to a collective form of contemplative, studious play. An example of the latter would be the occupation of Tiananmen Square in the 1980s. What is at stake here is defining occupation as the zone of contact between education and politics that displaces both: education becomes a public issue and politics loses its instrumental ends, becoming educational (a zone for contemplating its own conditions of possibility through the use of itself).

The failure to think politics and education has thus far been the result of trying to think the two in relation. For us, making public the occupation of infrastructure is precisely the point of contact between education and politics that displaces where education can happen and who can participate while at the same time revealing a new, noninstrumental politics that does not care to know what it is or where it is going, and is therefore happy (in and through the study of its own potentiality). If Agamben once argued that politics is the name for the "dimension in which works—linguistic and bodily, material and immaterial, biological and social—are deactivated and contemplated as such in order to liberate the inoperativity that has remained imprisoned in them,"[6] then contemplative educational practices like P4I are already in contact with radical politics through a shared logic of inoperativity. This final chapter will expose this deep contact point in order to expand the discussion beyond the brick-and-mortar schoolhouse. In particular the Tiananmen Square occupation will emerge as a paradigm (i.e., that which makes something intelligible) of a collective form of studious play through its use of linguistic and social potentialities. Such play is as infantile as it is anarchic and as anarchic as it is infantile. In this sense, the linguistic practices we have theorized in P4I can help clarify what is infantile in the political view of Tiananmen, while Tiananmen can help clarify the political in the educational view of infancy.

To explore these interconnected theses, we will have to shift away from the political story P4C tells about itself and its roots in American liberal, deliberative democracy.[7] Instead, we will have to situate P4I within the critical theory tradition. This is because Agamben locates his own project on this terrain, as emerging from within, problematizing, and developing certain ideas that are essential to this tradition yet somewhat foreign to the American liberal democratic, pluralistic, and pragmatist traditions. While some strands of P4C might also find themselves at home within critical theory,[8] we will not engage with this important literature in this conclusion. Instead, we will take up the problem of P4C from another angle outside usual discussions surrounding Peirce, Dewey, Rawls, and others in order to expose and develop the more anarchic political side of P4I.

The Context: Living the Learning Society

This analysis is urgent precisely because of the ways in which education and politics have dovetailed in recent years, forming the learning society. In the learning society, political relations become learning relations and vice versa. While we discussed the learning society in broad details in the Introduction, it is now time to return to this topic in order to clarify the backdrop against which we must think the practice of P4I as a contact point that suspends the operativity of the relation that is already circulating throughout society. A key argument proposed by critical theorists Michael Hardt and Antonio Negri is that capitalist expropriation is no longer restricted to the factory. Drawing on Marx's original theory of capitalist expansion during the industrial era, Hardt and Negri focus on a shift from formal to "real subsumption"[9] of social relations by capitalism. Whereas the former emphasizes expansion of capitalism the latter emphasizes intensification of its disciplinary forms of control. No longer is there an outside to capitalism needing to be colonized. Instead, social relations, communication systems, information networks, and affective modes of labor are all subsumed within capitalism. Social life as a whole becomes "immaterial labor"[10] for capitalist expropriation. Capitalism now operates through biopower, or a power that concerns the management of habits, affects, and social relationships. This notion of power undermines the classic Marxian distinction between the base and the superstructure, as the superstructure (culture, politics, and the social, broadly conceptualized) is now central to economic production (rather than mere ancillary reflections). The corollary of this thesis is that the industrial proletariat can no longer be *the* central and sovereign motor driving revolution, hence the centrality of the multitude outlined above. The working class cannot, in other words, be a stand-in for all other political movements and political concerns. The agents of revolution pluralize and multiply, but more interestingly, the locations of revolution out of bounds of the factory are potentially infinite. Or, perhaps more aptly, society itself has become a factory exploiting the immaterial labor of an underpaid and/or unpaid multitude of "employees."

The multitude of political actors is continually subsumed under forms of subjectivity resulting from the command and capture of Empire. These subjectivities include the indebted, the mediatized, the securitized, and the represented.[11] We agree with this list, but we find a major oversight in Hardt and Negri's work in this regard: the subjectivity of the lifelong learner. This is a subjectivity that is (a) continually indebted to institutions, (b) continually under threat of economic obsolescence, and (c) forced to become entrepreneurial by seeking out new skills needed to be seen as productive and efficient. Circling back to the question of the oath, we can say that the lifelong learner takes an oath to constantly search out options for self-learning in order to optimize his or her potentials for efficacy and productivity, but in so doing curses the life that does not live up to these expectations (essentially abandoning the self to a life of debt and guilt over this debt). If social life has become a factory for producing certain forms of subjectivity desirable to capitalist command and control, then so too has this very same social life become a *schoolhouse* full of entrepreneurial learners faced with the task of searching out learning opportunities to develop the skills and dispositions that are deemed as desirable by a fast-paced knowledge economy. Schooling is no longer restricted to the school; it expands outward until the world itself becomes the school. Learning and laboring thus emerge *together* as mutually reinforcing discourses and practices—learning economies and immaterial economies of affect, information, and knowledge can no longer be separated.

Indeed we might go so far as to argue that the learning society is a society that is predicated on the management (or government) of the *relationship* between learning and economic logics. In other words, relationality enables an *articulation* between these two spheres of life through various means-ends equations that can be assessed and evaluated according to specific criteria internal to the learning society. Relationality enables learning to become a means for the economy and vice versa, producing synergistic flows of subjects, immaterial labor, and knowledge between otherwise separate sectors. The result is an advanced form of communicative capitalism that appropriates the immaterial wealth of linguistic and social resources put into circulation between learning and laboring. In learning, capitalism finds its educational logic and exploits it to create increasingly flexible laborers for an immaterial, communicative-based knowledge economy. And in capitalism, learning finds its economic logic, which transforms personal development and skill maximization into future-oriented promises of returns on educational investments. As such, relationality concerns the functionality of two systems that operate through one another.

To suture the relation, communicative capitalism issues a *command*. A command, for Agamben, is an *arche* or that which "gives a beginning" and "is also what commands and governs [something's] growth, development, circulation, and transmission."[12] Communicative capitalism commands that people speak and that this speech becomes a commodity within an information economy. The command is an *arche* or order that founds and then governs speech, putting it in relation with various systems so as to ensure an economy of utterances for capitalist ends. In the context of the learning society, the economic *arche* insists that children speak and that such speech be reified as a representation of their aptitudes for later economization. These commands can take a number of forms including "Teach children for the economy of the future" or "Develop the soft skills to help students find jobs in the information economy." Here, the command creates an imperative from without to fashion relationships between schools and economic needs in such a way that education is instrumentalized. At the same time, the laws of learning command capitalism to orient itself toward the learnification of production in the form of continual assessment and testing of employees so as to manage skills and increase performance. In this sense, the commands between learnification and economization pass through one another, creating intricate relay points for multiple scalar relations to be produced. Perhaps more telling is how these commands are often given in such a way that liberal democracy conceals the learning-economic commands. Thus "Let your voice be heard!" can equally be read as a liberation of speech and as a mechanism of capture that enables the speech to be controlled, policed, or co-opted by a knowledge economy that thrives through the circulation of opinions and voices. In this sense, the liberal democratic command to "speak up!" that is so dominant in progressive, constructivist educational circles (including certain variants inspired by Lipman and Sharp) is yoked to a certain notion of economic viability that secures its hold over life by folding within itself human communicability as such.

Opposed to relational negotiation between the means and ends of learning and the economy, we are interested in *contact* that fundamentally suspends the logic of relationality. Instead of finding overlaps between existing means and ends in order to promote functional hybridization and output maximization, contact interjects an anomalous zone wherein existing means and ends are suspended, rendered inoperative, and opened up for free use that is not determined in advance. Contact takes up the infrastructure of the learning society as a pure means in suspension from the ends of the learning society, and in so doing deposes the command of communicative capitalism.

Given that the learning society collapses the space and time of the schoolhouse and of the economic and political spheres—transforming us all into lifelong learners who must learn the lessons taught by the economy as the ultimate teacher—we cannot postpone a discussion of P4I and politics. But this discussion is fraught with dangers as it is often the case that education becomes a mere means to a political end outside of itself, resulting in the instrumentalization of education. Thus our task is to think education and politics without falling into this trap. We will argue that the occupation of learning infrastructure—the infrastructure (as a pure means) that underlies and makes functional the learning society—is a way in which education and politics *contact* one another without the former being reduced to an instrument of the latter.

A Coming Politics

Although often referred to (rightly so) as an impolitical thinker, Agamben's work is driven by a certain political question: How can we ensure that Auschwitz does not happen again? We can see this play out in two political events that were formative for Agamben: the May '68 protests in Paris and the Tiananmen Square occupation in 1989. To understand why Agamben would see traditional politics as insufficient, it is important to point out that for him, the May '68 protests where, not just indirectly, but essentially, about the threat (and legacy) of totalitarianism, and the Holocaust, in particular. While in France, the emphasis of the protests was on established bureaucratic, political, and military elites, capitalism, and traditional institutions and values in general, in Germany, the student movement was to a significant degree a reaction to the continuation of officials in all areas of society—including in schools and universities—who had been active Nazis (targeting, for example, the president of Bonn University who had been involved in the building of concentration camps). Something similar could be said—although to a lesser degree—about France, with regard to the collaboration of the Vichy regime with Nazi Germany. While the Holocaust was only one of the issues and only in some countries, for Agamben, it could be said to have been of crucial importance, calling Auschwitz "the decisive lesson of the century."[13]

What the lesson of Auschwitz consisted in, for Agamben, is directly related to the insights he gained during his study of the law, as it allowed him to gauge the vastness of Auschwitz: "With the exception of occasional moments of lucidity," he writes, "it has taken almost half a century to understand that law did not exhaust the problem, but rather that the very problem was so enormous as to call into question law itself, dragging it to its own ruin."[14] In other words, for him, Auschwitz cannot be understood (and, thus, not opposed) in conventional legal or political terms. What this meant for his perspective on the events of May '68 was that he saw the politics of the student revolt as still operating within a legal framework (i.e., seeing conventional political measures and efforts to reform educational and other institutions as an adequate form of protest), whereas, for him, the fact that Auschwitz had been possible meant that politics had to be fundamentally rethought.

The event that led Agamben to eventually turn his focus toward politics, and, more specifically, toward the formulation of a response to the question of what kind of politics was still possible (or indeed necessary) after Auschwitz, were the 1989 protests in Beijing's Tiananmen Square that ended with a violent crackdown by the Chinese government. What made Tiananmen an example for a different (nonconventional) politics, for Agamben, was the kind of community that the protesters gathered in Tiananmen Square represented. In contrast to their French counterparts, two decades earlier, which Blanchot described as a "negative community," that is, a community mediated by a simple absence of conditions rather than by a condition of belonging, Agamben describes the community formed by the protesters in Tiananmen Square as a community mediated by belonging itself, meaning that the participants did not *belong to* a certain community but rather exhibited or displayed the potentiality to belong without content (identity or destiny).

What accounted for this difference, for Agamben, was that among the protesters in Tiananmen Square there was a "relative absence of determinate contents in their demands," given that "democracy and freedom are notions too generic and broadly defined to constitute the real object of a conflict, and the only concrete demand, the rehabilitation of Hu Yao-Bang, was immediately granted."[15] Instead, what prompted the violent crackdown, for Agamben, was that for the leaders there was nothing worse than an opposition without some kind of identity. What he saw was an example of a new kind of politics (a *coming politics*) that is no longer characterized by a "*struggle for the conquest or control of the State, but a struggle between the State and the non-State (humanity), an insurmountable disjunction between whatever singularity and the State organization.*"[16] As Agamben emphasizes, this is not the same as an opposition between the social and the State, given that "[w]hatever singularities cannot form a *societas* because they do not possess any identity to vindicate nor any bond of belonging for which to seek recognition." And he continues:

> In the final instance the State can recognize any claim for identity—even that of a State identity within the State. ... What the State cannot tolerate in any way, however, is that the singularities form a community without affirming an identity, that humans co-belong without any representable condition of belonging (even in the form of a simple presupposition).[17]

For Agamben, Tiananmen thus represents both a manifestation of a community in a positive sense (the fact that it is undefined makes it open to possibilities), while, for the same reason, representing the largest threat to—and the most effective safeguard against—dogmatism, totalitarianism, and oppression.

If Auschwitz was the decisive lesson of the century, what it taught us, we could say through Agamben, is that conventional forms of politics are not able to protect us from another Auschwitz (or a continuation of the conditions that made Auschwitz possible). But this poses an interesting problem for us. Although Agamben clearly articulates a coming politics, how do his remarks on Auschwitz and Tiananmen connect to his remarks on studious play, study, and contemplation? While not making any overt gesture in this direction, we would like to highlight a passage from *The Use of Bodies*, which is the last installment of the *Homo Sacer* series. At the very close of this final text, Agamben writes the following: "Contemplation and inoperativity are in this sense the metaphysical operators of anthropogenesis, which, in liberating living human beings from every biological and social destiny and every predetermined task, render them available for that peculiar absence of work that we are accustomed to calling 'politics' and 'art.'"[18] To summarize, contemplation (studious play) liberates humans by encouraging a certain form of anthropogenesis through the use of thought to think and speak its own coming into being (its own infancy), rendering human life "available" for politics. In this sense, contemplation and politics are necessarily *connected* through a shared inoperativity. Contemplation deactivates certain roles, beliefs, assumptions, biases, and world views by encouraging studious play with the preconditions of our subjective constitution just as politics deactivates human actions and works, opening them up for free use. The hinge that unites and separates the two is precisely inoperativity, and by extension, a returning to human potentiality.

If this is indeed the case, then we can return to the Tiananmen Square occupation with an eye toward how it not only embodies a coming politics but also and equally a coming education that made participants available for a political experiment with the time and space of its own self-constitution.

The Space and Time of Contact between Education and Politics

In this section we want to tease out the paradoxical contact zone between education and politics with explicit reference to the space and the time of inoperativity. What does such a zone look like? In particular, the space of contact is a weakly utopian occupation of infrastructure, and the time of contact is always contemporary. These two dimensions emerge when the function of the infrastructure supporting learning is suspended and the time of deferral (into the past or present) is deactivated and returned to the contemporary moment.

Space

There are essentially two ways to think about the underlying spatial model informing the politics on the Left. The first is the classical Marxist notion of politics as ultimately a struggle over the control of the economic base. On this view, there are certain, clearly prescribed and privileged political subjects of social emancipation: the proletariat. It is the *objective contradictions* existing between the interests of the proletariat and the bourgeoisie that define the political terrain of struggle. The kind of education internal to this model of politics concerns learning to see one's self as a member of a universal, revolutionary class (the proletariat). Thus the learning here is really about understanding one's objective position in the forces and relations of capitalist production and how this position also ascribes certain objective, material interests that can only be met through a total negation of class-based economic structures. A key reference point in this respect can be found in the writings of V.I. Lenin. Lenin writes,

> [I]t [the trade union] is not a *state organization; nor is it one designed for coercion*, but for education. It is an organization designed to draw in and to train; it is, in fact, a school: a school of administration, a school of economic management, a school of communism. It is a very unusual type of school, because there are not teachers or pupils; this is an extremely unusual combination of what has necessarily come down to us from capitalism, and what comes from the ranks of the advanced revolutionary detachments, which you might call the revolutionary vanguard of the proletariat.[19]

In short, the site of the school is displaced into the site of politics: the factory and its unionization. Through mobilization of the union, workers can come to recognize themselves as universal subjects of emancipation (revolutionary vanguard of the proletariat). Notice that this "very unusual" combination of education and politics comes down from capitalism itself, which, as we have discussed, has slowly displaced education from the schoolhouse into the factory and the factory into the school. But as much as this is reactionary, it is also revolutionary, coming down from "advanced revolutionary detachments." In other words, while the conditions of the factory that the workers find themselves within have been generated by capitalism, this has not precluded an appropriation of these conditions, now detached from their capitalist ends, for revolutionary advancement. Also notice that what has been appropriated from capitalism is not simply *any* educational displacement but specifically the law of learning. This learning lacks teachers and pupils, but it operates in terms of organizing means and ends. The union is a school that sets up a relationship between learning as an educational means to a political end (proletarian subjectification) within the schoolhouse of the factory. The factory no longer simply produces capitalist profits but also revolutionary subjectivity. In sum, education is (a) displaced (into the factory) and (b) instrumentalized (according to the laws of learning).

As the objectivity of class struggle was increasingly called into question throughout the twentieth century through the rise of a variety of nonclass-based struggles (around issues of gender, race, sexuality, and disability as they emerged in the aftermath of May '68), a new, post-Marxist emphasis on the question of symbolic *antagonism* emerged in the work of Ernesto Laclau and Chantal Mouffe.[20] The location of struggle shifted to the superstructural domain of rhetoric, semiotics, and discourse, and how signifiers come to be sutured together into a (counter) hegemonic formation. If politics is a struggle to network together signifiers, then it becomes increasingly diffused, relational, and differential. It is no longer prescribed to a fixed location (factories) and a fixed subject (industrial workers). Counter-hegemonic coalitions of different groups can be sutured together through the constitution of a chain of equivalences between different, particular groups around an empty signifier such as "justice" or "equality," which bring all the competing special interest groups together into a contingent and antagonistic bloc. Politics, on this model, is a collective investment into a common name that is capable of holding within itself (precisely because it is virtually empty) an expansive coalition. The goal here is to take symbolic, social, legal, and state power(s) through discursive struggle over the language of emancipation (whose voices are included/excluded).

Discourse is central to this understanding of politics, but as Laclau and Mouffe point out, discourse also is fundamentally *pedagogical* in nature in that it functions to change ways of thinking, imagining, and understanding[21] through the articulation of an "imaginary"[22] that networks together previously separated struggles. If classical Marxist education in trade unions reveals what capitalism conceals (the objective interests of the worker as proletariat), here post-Marxist education through discourse produces new subjects through articulation—subjects that are contingent and not guaranteed by laws of history. Nevertheless, similarities remain between the two approaches. In both cases, education is instrumentalized for the sake of political ends. While the first concerns revolution and the second expansion of democratic rights, the point for us is that education is oriented toward certain predetermined functions within a set of contradictions or antagonisms. Second, as with classical Marxism, the model of education here is learning, which lends itself to such means-end thinking. In short, both Marxism and post-Marxism concern the construction of *relations* between learning and politics. And in this sense, they reproduce the essential logic of articulation found within capitalism (and maximized in communicative capitalism).

This is not to deny that there are benefits to both positions outlined above, and there have been historical payoffs for constructing revolutionary and counter-hegemonic relations between learning and politics. But we want to ask a different question—not one based on relationality but on contact. What kind of contact between education and politics becomes possible if we shift *location* of the problematic from the economic base or discursive superstructure to the space of *infrastructure*? Hardt and Negri's theory of the common as a positive production of immaterial labor (language, affects, habits, and so forth) from below is one possible starting point for theorizing a politics of infrastructure,[23] but here we want to focus on another possible entry point: Agamben's theory of gestures (as a kind of bodily infrastructure). The space of gesture is, as Agamben highlights, a space of pure mediality.[24] We can see gestures in the dancing or playing or contemplating body where movement shows itself moving or thinking shows itself thinking. And in showing themselves, movement and thought become open to free use. So too with infrastructure, which is the basic supporting *space* of economic production and *praxis*. By infrastructure, we mean material and immaterial (linguistic) means that make action and work possible. While one might think that the struggle over the economic base in classical Marxism concerns infrastructure (in the form of the relations and forces of production), we would argue that this approach already places means in relation to ends, inscribing within them a predetermined functionality (productivity). The same can be said of post-Marxism, which already prescribes a certain function to the empty signifier (which, we might add in passing is a *negative* basis of politics, rather than an affirmative and positive one) within a hegemonic struggle and also prescribes a certain rhetorical *form* to this struggle (the chain of horizontal equivalences organized around a central emptiness that can only ever be partially filled). The question of classical Marxism is not about the relation between means and ends but rather about who controls this relationship in the first place (and how it can thus be exploited for private rather than public gains). Likewise, post-Marxist approaches to discourse always presuppose the speakability of language (its infancy) as destined for antagonist purposes (be they conservative or progressive). Our point is that these approaches fail to theorize the means (infrastructure) as such and therefore repeat the ancient Aristotelian bias that favors actions, ends, and actualization over and above potentiality. Politics deploys gestures, commanding them to take on certain operative forms within economic production or discursive action. An impolitical politics, on the other hand, would not deploy gestures but rather exhibit them as such. It would not try to optimize (take advantage of) infrastructure so much as render its operativity inoperative, put it out of work, in order to see what kinds of uses become possible beyond the material laws of history (Marxism) or the discursive laws of hegemonic struggle (post-Marxism).

With the shift from Marxism to post-Marxism, we find a broadening of the spaces where politics can happen (and *must* happen). We do not critique this trend toward expanding the political horizon. Instead, we want to claim that it does not go far enough. For post-Marxists, hegemonic antagonism takes place with relation to juridical and state institutions and is primarily oriented toward rights to expand democracy within constituted forms. Yet, as articulated by Agamben, it is not clear that state-oriented counter-hegemonic discourses (calling for the expansion of civil rights) are an adequate response to the current state of exception exemplified by the extra-juridical status of those spheres operating outside the law (to preserve the law). These conditions necessitate a different space for politics—one that is not strictly oriented toward the economic base or the legal/state superstructure. Such a politics would be out-of-bounds of the spaces of Marxist and post-Marxist conceptual frameworks, and in this sense, be largely invisible, or non-political (impolitical).

Time

The space of inoperativity is also always contemporary. As Agamben argues, the contemporary moment is not a mere point in a chronological, linear organization of time. Instead, it is a rupture that is characterized by a "disconnection" and "anachronism."[25] To be truly contemporary, one does not belong to their time, adjusting a form-of-life to certain social norms and values. Instead, the contemporary person is more or less "irrelevant"[26] to those around them precisely because they seem out of joint or untimely. In this sense, the contemporary is a temporal moment of *noncoincidence* with one's time that, precisely because of this condition, enables an individual to *contemplate* time. Tiananmen was a contemporary occupation precisely because it was untimely, opening up a fissure in the present for occupants to contemplate a coming politics (a politics without an identity or a destiny). It was neither a flash from the past (as in a nostalgic return to that which has been lost) nor simply a utopian projection into a future (as the negation of what exists in the present). Instead, it was "no more" in the present while "not yet" in the future. What was unleashed was a temporal contact point between "what is" and "what is to come" that defines the peculiar nature of all potentiality. If this is correct, then as a consequence we can say that politics in Marxism and post-Marxism is *never in contact with the present*, is *never contemporary*. Instead, it merely *negates* the present in the name of a future to come.

In sum, Agamben's notion of an impolitical politics does not struggle over economic relations (by raising class consciousness) or over superstructural legal/juridical discourses of civil society (by creating the conditions for democratic speech) but rather exposes a more basic infrastructure that supports production, action, and works. This infrastructure is the *common space* of potentiality, with infancy being the name for the common space of potentiality in language. It is also the *contemporary time* of the present moment released from teleological ends always posited in a deferred future to come or a past needing redemption. The infrastructure of language is (a) common and (b) always already in use and thus contemporary (as use is never to come but also about becoming in the present moment of auto-affection). It can be appropriated and made to function according to specific teleological commands, but *ontologically* speaking, infrastructure is first and foremost free and open for use (as with Agamben's analysis of gestures). Occupying the common space and contemporary time of infrastructure returns politics to use. Such use does not assume a specific space for the appearance of the political, nor does it prescribe a particular actor, nor does it necessitate a specific orientation/end. Instead, this use is unbound as much as it is out-of-bounds of Marxism and post-Marxism.

Returning to Tiananmen, we can now rethink Agamben's example of a coming politics to see how it is also a contact point between politics and education that is not instrumental. Our rereading highlights how politics and education pass through one another via a space and time of inoperativity opened up through occupation of infrastructure.

The Tiananmen Square occupation offered a fleeting image of what happens when the suspension of infrastructure through studious play becomes a public concern, revealing a different space of politics outside economic or statist/legal struggles. In this case, the coming community occupied a space in the heart of Beijing, a space of great symbolic power for the Communist Party and for the identity of the state—a space where citizens *learn* how to be Communists, a space dominated by the command of the party to behave in a certain way. Once occupied, this law of learning was suspended, opening the space up to new kinds of experiences that were not strictly reducible to either education or politics but rather exposed the contact between the two. Notice, the space of the coming community was not *outside* or *over there* in a utopian displacement. Rather it was right in the middle of the city where action happens and where civic learning displays itself. But instead of turning the space into a space for a protest movement, the space was rendered inoperative through durational occupation, and in turn, its learning function was deactivated (as a space for civic instruction by the Party). The result was a studious community defining itself by its own rules of self-formation through experiments in living together rather than a protest movement defined by a clear identity and a clear political or economic agenda. What was so frustrating for the Chinese Communist Party was that the space no longer *taught* citizens how to be or who they were, and, in turn, there was *nothing to learn* from the coming community about what kinds of concessions the state ought to give in order for life to return to normal. Instead, the community was simply whatever it was and preferred not to teach or learn but rather contemplate its own potentiality to be thusly. And in doing so, it made its studious play with its own potentiality a public, and by extension, political concern.

The demand that Tiananmen responded to was *internal* to itself, internal to its constitution of itself through the use of itself. Thus Tiananmen can be interpreted as studious play with its potentiality to become this or that kind of social body, figuring out how to use its awkward linguistic and social gestures as it played with them. As such, the infantile demand for self-constitution was *contemporary* to the emergence of the multitude in the square. It was not predetermined ahead of time as in the Marxian model by the laws of history calling forth a specific set of political actors (the proletariat). And it was not a demand that was oriented *away* from itself toward a specific constituted institution (such as the state of a juridical apparatus) as in the post-Marxist model. While the law of history *places* a demand on certain political actors from the *past* (as it is inscribed in the forces and relations of production), the post-Marxist model of discourse projects the demand of participants *outward*, away from itself toward an institutional body, in the hopes of *future* political gains. In the former, the worker learns to be a proletariat (and thus justifies past losses by taking up the mantel of revolutionary action), and in the second, the state learns of the demands of the marginalized (and thus negotiates for hegemonic reform in the future). In both cases, the kind of relation between learning and politics always misses the contemporary moment. When a demand emerges from within a collective's use of itself to constitute itself in its infancy, then the demand institutes a *contemporary* point of contact between education and politics in the form of study now made into a public concern (and thus containing a certain political dimension, even if this dimension is invisible to traditional political paradigms).

When occupation of the space and time of infrastructure becomes a public concern (as in Tiananmen), then a contact point erupts between contemplation and politics, often times with ambiguous results that do not satisfy either the educational establishment (as it is unclear what the outcomes are or what is learned) or political activists (who want to transform studious communities into political movements with a clear identity and agenda that can teach those in power). While critique from educationalists and political activists is not in itself misguided (and certainly there is more than enough room for these perspectives), all we want to point out is that perhaps jumping to these more or less instrumental approaches to the education-politics articulation misses what is most singular and unique about occupation of infrastructure: that it is a space of infancy and use. Politics and education thus contact each other when they *lose* each other through mutual occupation (and thus exodus from preexisting functionality). Politics and education can therefore only be thought as a kind of relational non-relation or a relation that functions only in so far as it renders nonfunctional the identities put in relation in the first place. And in this sense, a coming education (one that is contemplative, playfully studious) can and does make available a coming politics: weakly utopian (everywhere and thus nowhere in particular) and contemporary.

P4I as a Contact Point

Turning to P4I, we can now see how it offers a certain contact point between education and politics that does not collapse one into the other but rather situates itself in a kind of exodus that suspends the identities of both at their mutual point of potentialization. For instance, the paradoxical time of P4I no longer functions according to the instrumentalized and functionalized temporality of school clock time (where each second is dominated by a disciplinary law of efficiency), yet it is not yet outside the time of education. Stated differently, it is not learning time (which is always on the clock), but rather study time, or the time that remains when the clock stops and when the teacher allows students to respond to the demand to babble (play with language).

In terms of space, we can think of P4I as the space opened up and sustained by a certain demand (i.e., the demand to speak, created by the silence of the Voice of the teacher). As stated above, relationality presupposes two, distinct, predefined identities that must negotiate what, who, and how they are with regards to one another. The relationship between learning and the communicative, knowledge economy of liberal democracies is best articulated in terms of the command. Another way of stating this is that communicative capitalism *commands* that we speak. A command is a non-apophantic imperative that is, for Agamben, linked directly to law, religion, and magic. All three of these discourses operate with an injunction in mind (think here of the Ten Commandments in Christianity). In the current historical moment, Agamben finds the ontology of the command gaining increasing prevalence. For instance, the imperative of communicative capitalism is "Speak!" It does not care *what* is spoken, but rather *that* speaking must happen (regardless of content). In this sense, what is captured by capitalism is speakability itself. And this is most pernicious in liberal democratic societies. As Agamben writes,

> I believe that a good description of the so-called democratic societies in which we live consists in defining them as societies in which the ontology of the command has taken the place of the ontology of the assertion, yet not in the clear form of an imperative but in the more underhanded form of advice, of invitation, of the warning given in the name of security, in such a way that obedience to a command takes the form of a cooperation and, often, of a command given to oneself.[27]

The liberal democratic command is to "freely" speak one's mind and put one's speech in circulation. This command is covert as it comes disguised as one's autonomous choice rather than an external imposition. The relation between economy and learning is precisely this command. Indeed, we might go so far as to suggest that the problem with P4C (as envisioned by Sharp at the outset of this chapter) is not that it is not democratic enough but that it is *too* democratic, meaning that it reflects back the command of the communicative, knowledge economy.[28] The learning society is precisely a society of commands where individuals as entrepreneurs learn to speak for themselves. In turn, this freedom to speak necessitates the management and government of speech acts by individuals as self-regulating, democratic subjects.

But if this is the case, how is P4I any different? Like P4C, P4I also concerns speaking, and it would appear at the outset that it also reiterates the basic tenets of the communicative, knowledge economy. Yet there is a significant difference. Agamben writes, "The spectacle [of communicative capitalism] still contains something like a positive possibility—and it is our task to use this possibility against it."[29] Because communicability has been thrown into relief by capitalism's appetite, it can now be struggled over, and in this sense, the greatest darkness becomes an opportunity. Agamben summarizes, "But exactly for this reason, the age in which we live is also that in which for the first time it becomes possible for human beings to experience their own linguistic essence—to experience, that is, not some language content or some true propositions, but language *itself*, as well as the very fact of speaking."[30] On our reading, the appropriation of language in the current moment is not purely negative but actually unleashes the conditions necessary for us to playfully study language as a pure means, as social infrastructure. To do so means we have to suspend the relationality of education and economy of liberal democracies via the command and, instead, recognize a contact point between education and politics in the form of the *demand*.

Drawing on Chapter 1 of this book but placing it in a political context, we argue that while a command is always to speak (and in a sense take an oath to speak and speak well!), a demand is to return to the very conditions of speakability. It is not actually an imperative (neither extrinsic nor intrinsic) but much more akin to an apophantic statement that says, "Language is!" In this sense, the demand does not command (in terms of oath taking, cursing, or blessing). Instead, it reminds us that language is our common infrastructure, and that it is this infrastructure that is to be wrestled with (more so than any debate concerning what to say or how to say it).

As such, the demand of P4I is not that we make language function better (so that it becomes more reasonable and more deliberative according to democratic ends), but rather that we are reminded that language as such—as infrastructure—is what is most common and what is most at risk. The demand returns us to the *common space and time* of language that we all belong to without belonging to anything in particular. This space and time is without command (*arche*) and is thus inherently *an-arche* or anarchistic (without law, without oath, without command). Politics and education meet at this anarchic contact point where each is undestined. Agamben's notion of infancy is, as he reminds us, a "common power"[31] underlying any and every act of communication, every specific language game, and every mother tongue. Indeed, any communication is, for Agamben, "first of all communication not of something in common but of communicability itself"[32] as this common power. P4I is a sharing with friends this common power in a space of being-thus. It is not *for* the development, growth, or progress toward a particular notion of a political life or in accordance with a predetermined law of reasonableness. Instead it is a form-of-life that is infantile, meaning without foundations and without destiny. In the end, infancy is anarchic and anarchy is infantile (in that both are impotential remnants that depose the law).

Perhaps we can summarize P4I with as simple procedural demand: *Let children use language (babble), and through that use rediscover what is most common (infancy) and thus without law (anarchic).* "Anarchic" in this context refers to a form-of-life that is (a) without negative foundation and (b) without destiny. Anarchism is the contact zone between education and politics wherein the functioning of infrastructure is rendered inoperative and opened up for common use. Of course, this impolitical education and educational politics might seem strange as it does not critique the mode of production or the division of labor. Nor does it build up counter-hegemonic, democratic knowledge through the construction of chains of equivalence between disparate identities.

At the same time, it is not reducible to a post-critical lineage either.³³ Instead, we conclude that it is *pre-critical* in that it exposes students to the free use of language as infrastructure that supports (without being absorbed and exhausted by) critical or post-critical endeavors. It is time that this infrastructure itself be seen for what it is: a pure means that enables us to finally contact the potentiality that subtends all binaries separating education from politics in the first place.

Notes

Introduction

1. See Gert J.J. Biesta, *Beyond Learning: Democratic Education for a Human Future* (Boulder, CO: Paradigm Publishers, 2006); Maarten Simons and Jan Masschelein, "The Learning Society and Governmentality: An Introduction," *Educational Philosophy and Theory*, vol. 38, no. 4 (2006): 417–30; Maarten Simons, "Learning as Investment: Notes on Governmentality and Biopolitics," *Educational Philosophy and Theory*, vol. 38, no. 4 (2006): 523–40; Tyson E. Lewis, *On Study: Giorgio Agamben and Educational Potentiality* (New York: Routledge, 2013); Tyson E. Lewis, *Inoperative Learning: A Radical Rewriting of Educational Potentialities* (New York: Routledge, 2017).
2. Biesta, *Beyond Learning*, 20.
3. Lewis, *Inoperative Learning*.
4. Matthew Lipman, Ann Margaret Sharp, and Fredrick S. Oscanyan, *Philosophy in the Classroom* (Philadelphia: Temple University Press, 1980).
5. Matthew Lipman, *Thinking in Education* (New York: Cambridge University Press, 2003), 18–19.
6. Lipman, *Thinking in Education*, 83.
7. Lipman, *Philosophy Goes to School* (Philadelphia: Temple University Press, 1988), 42.
8. Ann Margaret Sharp, *In Community of Inquiry with Ann Margaret Sharp: Childhood, Philosophy and Education*, ed. Maughn Rollins Gregory and Megan Jane Laverty (New York: Routledge, 2017), 53.
9. Sharp, *In Community of Inquiry*, 55.
10. See Lipman, *Thinking in Education*.
11. See Nancy Vansieleghem, "Philosophy as the Wind for Thinking," *Journal of Philosophy of Education*, vol. 39, no. 1 (2005): 19–37; Karin Saskia Murris, "Philosophy with Children, the Stingray and the Educative Value of Disequilibrium," *Journal of Philosophy of Education*, vol. 42, no. 3–4 (2008): 667–85; Gert Biesta, "Philosophy, Exposure, and Children: How to Avoid the Instrumentalization of Philosophy in Education," in *Philosophy for Children in Transition: Problems and Prospects*, ed. Nancy Vansieleghem and David Kennedy (Malden, MA: Wiley, 2012); Thomas Storme and Joris Vlieghe, "The Experience of Childhood and the Learning Society," in *Philosophy for Children in*

Transition: Problems and Prospects, ed. Nancy Vansieleghem and David Kennedy (Malden, MA: Wiley, 2012); Nancy Vansieleghem, "Philosophy with Children as an Exercise in Parrhesia: An Account of a Philosophical Experiment with Children in Cambodia," in *Philosophy for Children in Transition: Problems and Prospects*, ed. Nancy Vansieleghem and David Kennedy (Malden, MA: Wiley, 2012).

12 Biesta, "Philosophy, Exposure, and Children," 142.
13 Biesta, "Philosophy, Exposure, and Children," 149–50.
14 Vansieleghem, "Philosophy with Children as an Exercise in Parrhesia," 165.
15 Storme and Vlieghe, "The Experience of Childhood," 26.
16 Alina Reznitskaya and Richard C. Anderson, "Analyzing Argumentation in Rich, Natural Contexts," *Informal Logic*, vol. 26, no. 2 (2006): 175–98; Alina Reznitskaya and Ian A.G. Wilkinson, *The Most Reasonable Answer: Helping Students Build Better Arguments Together* (Cambridge, MA: Harvard University Press, 2017).
17 Alina Reznitskaya, Monica Glina, Brian Carolan, Olivier Michaud, Jon Rogers, Lavina Sequeira, "Examining Transfer Effects from Dialogic Discussions to New Tasks and Contexts," *Contemporary Educational Psychology*, no. 37 (2012): 288.
18 Giorgio Agamben, *The Time That Remains: A Commentary on the Letter to the Romans*, trans. Patricia Dailey (Stanford: Stanford University Press, 2005), 69.
19 See Nancy Vansieleghem and David Kennedy, "What Is Philosophy for Children, What Is Philosophy *with* Children—After Matthew Lipman?" in *Philosophy for Children in Transition: Problems and Prospects*, ed. Nancy Vansieleghem and David Kennedy (Malden: Wiley, 2012).
20 Walter Omar Kohan, *Childhood, Education and Philosophy: New Ideas for an Old Relationship* (New York: Routledge, 2014).
21 Tyson E. Lewis, *On Study: Giorgio Agamben and Educational Potentiality* (London: Routledge, 2013).
22 Lipman, *Philosophy Goes to School*.
23 Gareth Matthews, *Philosophy & the Young Child* (Cambridge, MA: Harvard University Press, 1982).
24 Giorgio Agamben, *Infancy and History: The Destruction of Experience*, trans. Liz Heron (London: Verso, 1993), 6.
25 Agamben, *Infancy and History*, 10.
26 Giorgio Agamben, *Potentialities: Collected Essays in Philosophy*, trans. Daniel Heller-Roazen (Stanford: Stanford University Press, 1999), 182.
27 Agamben, *Potentialities*, 183.
28 Lipman, *Philosophy Goes to School*, 27.
29 Agamben, *Potentialities*, 67.
30 Lipman, *Philosophy Goes to School*, 40.
31 Agamben, *Potentialities*, 91.
32 Agamben, *Potentialities*, 100.

33 Lipman, *Philosophy Goes to School*, 28.
34 Giorgio Agamben, *The Use of Bodies*, trans. Adam Kotsko (Stanford: Stanford University Press, 2014), 51.
35 Lipman, *Philosophy Goes to School*, 100–1.
36 Lipman, *Thinking in Education*, 19.
37 Ann Margaret Sharp and Megan Jane Laverty, "Looking at Others' Faces," in *In Community of Inquiry with Ann Margaret Sharp: Childhood, Philosophy and Education*, ed. Maughn Rollins Gregory and Megan Jane Laverty (New York: Routledge, 2017).
38 Clive Lindop, "Harry 17: Judgment, Perspective and Philosophy," *Thinking: The Journal of Philosophy for Children*, vol. 8, no. 3 (1989): 39–40.
39 Lipman, *Philosophy Goes to School*, 38.

Chapter 1

1 Ivan Illich, *Deschooling Society* (London: Marion Boyars, 1970), 37.
2 Illich, *Deschooling Society*, 47.
3 Illich, *Deschooling Society*, 3.
4 Jan Masschelein and Maarten Simons, "School as Architecture for New Comers and Strangers: The Perfect School as Public School?" *Teachers College Record*, vol. 12, no. 2 (2010): 535–55.
5 Giorgio Agamben, *The Sacrament of Language: An Archeology of the Oath*, trans. Adam Kotsko (Stanford: Stanford University Press, 2011).
6 Agamben, *Sacrament of Language*, 66.
7 JanMasschelein, Jan and Maarten Simons, *In Defense of the School: A Public Issue*, trans. Jack McMartin (Leuven: E-ducation, Culture, & Society, 2013).
8 Olivier Michaud and Riku Välitalo, "Authority, Democracy and Philosophy: The Nature and Role of Authority in a Community of Philosophical Inquiry," in *The Routledge International Handbook of Philosophy for Children*, ed. Maughn Rollins Gregory, Joanna Haynes, and Karin Murris (London: Routledge, 2017), 29.
9 Giorgio Agamben, *Language and Death: The Place of Negativity*, trans. Karen Pinkus and Michael Hardt (Minneapolis: University of Minnesota Press, 2006), 59.
10 Agamben, *Language and Death*, 60.
11 Agamben, *Language and Death*, 62.
12 Agamben, *Language and Death*, 81.
13 Agamben, *Language and Death*, 95.
14 Agamben, *Language and Death*, 103.
15 Agamben, *The Sacrament of Language*, 3.
16 Agamben, *Sacrament of Language*, 4.

17 Agamben, *Sacrament of Language*, 8.
18 Agamben, *Sacrament of Language*, 11.
19 Agamben, *Sacrament of Language*, 30.
20 Agamben, *Sacrament of Language*, 31.
21 Agamben, *Sacrament of Language*, 44.
22 Agamben, *Sacrament of Language*, 43.
23 Agamben, *Sacrament of Language*, 69.
24 Giorgio Agamben, *Homo Sacer: Sovereign Power and Bare Life*, trans. Daniel Heller-Roazen (Stanford: Stanford University Press, 1998).
25 Jodi Dean, *Democracy and Other Neoliberal Fantasies: Communicative Capitalism and Left Politics* (Durham: Duke University Press, 2009).
26 Giorgio Agamben, *The Coming Community*, trans. Michael Hardt (Minneapolis: University of Minnesota Press, 1993), 80.
27 Agamben, *Sacrament of Language*, 72.
28 Agamben, *Sacrament of Language*, 72.
29 Agamben, *Coming Community*, 80.
30 Agamben, *Sacrament of Language*, 30.
31 Matthew Lipman, "Pixie and the Relationship between Cognitive Modelling and Cognitive Practice," in *Studies in Philosophy for Children: Pixie*, ed. Ronald F. Reed and Ann Margaret Sharp (Madrid: Ediciones de la Torre, 1996), 35.
32 Maughn Rollins Gregory (ed.), *Philosophy for Children Practitioner Handbook* (Montclair: IAPC, 2008), 10.
33 Giorgio Agamben, *What Is Philosophy?* trans. Lorenzo Chiesa (Stanford: Stanford University Press, 2018), 33.
34 Agamben, *What Is Philosophy?* 34.
35 Agamben, *The Use of Bodies*, trans. Adam Kotsko (Stanford: Stanford University Press, 2014), 51.
36 Cited in Giorgio Agamben, *The Fire and the Tale*, trans. Lorenzo Chiesa (Stanford: Stanford University Press, 2017), 29.
37 Agamben, *Fire and Tale*, 32.
38 Matthew Lipman, *Philosophy Goes to School* (Philadelphia: Temple University Press, 1988), 102.

Chapter 2

1 David Kennedy, *Philosophical Dialogue with Children: Essays on Theory and Practice* (Lewiston, NY: Edwin Mellen Press, 2010); Walter Omar Kohan, *Philosophy and Childhood: Critical Perspectives and Affirmative Practices* (New York: Palgrave, 2014).

2   Nancy Vansieleghem, "Philosophy with Children as an Exercise in Parrhesia: An Account of a Philosophical Experiment with Children in Cambodia," in *Philosophy for Children in Transition: Problems and Prospects*, ed. Nancy Vansieleghem and David Kennedy (Malden: Wiley, 2012).
3   Matthew Lipman, Ann Margaret Sharp, and Fredrick S. Oscanyan, *Philosophy in the Classroom* (Philadelphia: Temple University Press, 1980), 45.
4   Mario Biggeri and Marina Santi, "The Missing Dimensions of Children's Well-being and Well-becoming in Education Systems: Capabilities and Philosophy for Children," *Journal of Human Development and Capabilities*, vol. 13, no. 3 (2012): 373–95.
5   Thomas Jackson, "Philosophical Rules of Engagement," in *Philosophy in Schools: An Introduction for Philosophers and Teachers*, ed. S. Goering, N. Shudak, and T. Wartenberg (New York: Routledge, 2013).
6   Kennedy, *Philosophical Dialogue with Children*, 148, 173.
7   Matthew Lipman, *Philosophy Goes to School* (Philadelphia: Temple University Press, 1988), 107.
8   Lipman, *Philosophy Goes to School*, 108.
9   Maughn Rollins Gregory, Joanna Haynes, and Karin Murris, "Editorial Introduction: Philosophy for Children: An Educational and Philosophical Movement," in *The Routledge International Handbook of Philosophy for Children*, ed. Maughn Rollins Gregory, Joanna Haynes, and Karin Murris (London: Routledge, 2017), xxviii–ix.
10 Giorgio Agamben, *Homo Sacer: Sovereign Power and Bare Life*, trans. Daniel Heller-Roazen (Stanford: Stanford University Press, 1998), 51.
11 Agamben, *Homo Sacer*, 52.
12 Agamben, *Homo Sacer*, 50.
13 Agamben, *Homo Sacer*, 53.
14 Agamben, *Homo Sacer*, 55.
15 Giorgio Agamben, *The Highest Poverty: Monastic Rules and Form-of-Life*, trans. Adam Kotsko (Stanford: Stanford University Press, 2013), 46.
16 Agamben, *The Highest Poverty*, 121, 110.
17 Agamben, *The Highest Poverty*, 69.
18 Agamben, *The Highest Poverty*, 102.
19 Agamben, *The Highest Poverty*, 71.
20 Ann Margaret Sharp, *In Community of Inquiry with Ann Margaret Sharp: Childhood, Philosophy and Education*, ed. Maughn Rollins Gregory and Megan Jane Laverty (New York: Routledge, 2017), 239.
21 Kennedy, *Philosophical Dialogue with Children*, 110.
22 Matthew Lipman, *Thinking in Education* (New York: Cambridge University Press, 2003), 92.

23 Lipman, *Philosophy Goes to School*, 168.
24 Nadia Kennedy and David Kennedy, "Community of Philosophical Inquiry as a Discursive Structure and Its Role in School Curriculum Design," *Journal of Philosophy of Education*, vol. 45, no. 2 (2011): 265–83.
25 Giorgio Agamben, *The Use of Bodies*, trans. Adam Kotsko (Stanford: Stanford University Press, 2014), 63.
26 Agamben, *Use of Bodies*, 247.
27 Giorgio Agamben, *The Coming Community*, trans. Michael Hardt (Minneapolis: University of Minnesota Press, 1993), 90.
28 Agamben, *Coming Community*, 97.
29 Tyson E. Lewis, "The School as an Exceptional Space: Rethinking Education from the Perspective of the Biopedagogical," *Educational Theory*, vol. 56, no. 2 (2006), 159–76.
30 Agamben, *The Highest Poverty*, 111.

Chapter 3

1   Matthew Lipman, *Philosophy Goes to School* (Philadelphia, PA: Temple University Press, 1988), 28.
2   Matthew Lipman, Ann Margaret Sharp, and Fredrick S. Oscanyan, *Philosophy in the Classroom* (Philadelphia: Temple University Press, 1980), 9–10.
3   Lipman, *Philosophy Goes to School*, 24.
4   Ann Margaret Sharp, *In Community of Inquiry with Ann Margaret Sharp: Childhood, Philosophy and Education*, ed. Maughn Rollins Gregory and Megan Jane Laverty (New York: Routledge, 2017), 175.
5   Lipman, *Philosophy Goes to School*, 24.
6   Sharp, *In Community of Inquiry with Ann Margaret Sharp*, 177.
7   Giorgio Agamben, *End of the Poem: Studies in Poetics*, trans. Daniel Heller-Roazen (Stanford: Stanford University Press, 1999), 63.
8   Agamben, *End of the Poem*, 64.
9   Agamben, *End of the Poem*, 66.
10 Agamben, *End of the Poem*, 71.
11 Agamben, *End of the Poem*, 75.
12 Giorgio Agamben, *Infancy and History: On the Destruction of Experience*, trans. Liz Heron (London: Verso, 2007), 60.
13 Giorgio Agamben, *Means without End: Notes on Politics*, trans. Vicenzo Binetti and Cesare Casarino (Minneapolis: University of Minnesota Press, 2000), 70.
14 Matthew Lipman and Ann Margaret Sharp, "Some Educational Presuppositions for Philosophy for Children," *Oxford Review of Education*, vol. 4, no. 11 (1978): 90.

15 Matthew Lipman, *Thinking in Education* (Cambridge: Cambridge University Press, 1991), 2.
16 Agamben, *Infancy and History*, 77.
17 Giorgio Agamben, *Profanations*, trans. Jeff Fort (London: Zone Books, 2007), 76, 85.
18 Agamben, *Infancy and History*, 92.
19 Agamben, *Profanations*, 76.
20 Giorgio Agamben, *The State of Exception*, trans. Kevin Attell (Chicago: University of Chicago Press, 2005), 63.
21 Agamben, *State of Exception*, 63.
22 Giorgio Agamben, *The Adventure*, trans. Lorenzo Chiesa (Cambridge: MIT Press, 2018), 27.
23 Agamben, *Adventure*, 29.
24 Agamben, *Adventure*, 69.
25 Agamben, *Adventure*, 70.
26 Agamben, *Adventure*, 71.
27 Lipman, *Thinking in Education*, 84.
28 Agamben, *Adventure*, 82.
29 Giorgio Agamben, *Nudities*, trans. David Kishik and Stefan Pedatella (Stanford: Stanford University Press, 2010), 114.
30 Agamben, *Infancy and History*, 70.
31 Agamben, *Infancy and History*, 70.
32 Agamben, *Infancy and History*, 70.
33 Agamben, *Adventure*, 73.

Chapter 4

1 Matthew Lipman, *Thinking in Education* (New York: Cambridge University Press, 2003), 96.
2 Paulo Freire, *Pedagogy of the Oppressed*, trans. Myra Bergman Ramos (New York: Continuum, 2001); bell hooks, *Teaching to Transgress: Education as the Practice of Freedom* (New York: Routledge, 1994); Peter McLauren, *Che Guevara, Paulo Freire, and the Pedagogy of Revolution* (London: Rowan & Littlefield Publishers, 2000); Antonia Darder, *Reinventing Paulo Freire: A Pedagogy of Love* (New York: Routledge, 2017); Joris Vlieghe and Piotr Zamojski, *Toward an Ontology of Teaching: Thing-Centered Pedagogy, Affirmation, and Love for the World* (Rotterdam: Springer, 2019).
3 David Kennedy, "The Five Communities," *Analytic Teaching*, vol. 15, no. 1 (1994): 3–16.

4   Kennedy, "The Five Communities," 8.
5   Matthew Lipman, *Philosophy Goes to School* (Philadelphia, PA: Temple University Press, 1988), 42.
6   Not unlike the project articulated by Vlieghe and Zamojski in *Toward an Ontology of Teaching*.
7   Freire, *Pedagogy of the Oppressed*, 61, 62.
8   Freire, *Pedagogy of the Oppressed*, 63.
9   Paulo Freire, *Pedagogy of Freedom: Ethics, Democracy, and Civic Courage*, trans. Patrick Clarke (Lanham: Rowan and Littlefield, 2000).
10 Freire, *Pedagogy of the Oppressed*, 43.
11 Freire, *Pedagogy of the Oppressed*, 47.
12 Walter Omar Kohan, "Childhood, Education and Philosophy: Notes on Deterritorialisation," in *Philosophy for Children in Transition: Problems and Prospects*, ed. Nancy Vanieleghem and David Kennedy (Walden, MA: Wiley-Blackwell, 2012), 170.
13 Giorgio Agamben, *The Coming Community*, trans. Micahel Hardt (Minneapolis: University of Minnesota Press, 1993), 2.
14 Agamben, *Coming Community*, 67.
15 Agamben, *Coming Community*, 35.
16 Agamben, *Coming Community*, 36.
17 Agamben, *Coming Community*, 55.
18 Agamben, *Coming Community*, 67.
19 Agamben, *Coming Community*, 67.
20 Giorgio Agamben, *Creation and Anarchy: The Work of Art and the Religion of Capitalism*, trans. Adam Kotsko (Stanford: Stanford University press, 2019), 42.
21 Agamben, *Creation and Anarchy*, 45.
22 Giorgio Agamben, *The Use of Bodies*, trans. Adam Kotsko (Stanford: Stanford University Press, 2014), 172.
23 Agamben, *Use of Bodies*, 224.
24 Jonathan Cott, *Conversations with Glenn Gould* (Chicago: University of Chicago Press, 2005), 44.
25 Jeremy Siepmann, "Glenn Gould and the Interpreter's Prerogative," *The Musical Times*, vol. 131, no. 1763 (1990): 27.
26 Agamben, *Coming Community*, 28–9.
27 Agamben, *Coming Community*, 89.
28 Giorgio Agamben, *The Time That Remains: A Commentary on the Letter to the Romans*, trans. Patricia Dailey (Stanford: Stanford University Press, 2005), 128.
29 Agamben, *Time That Remains*, 128.
30 Giorgio Agamben, *What Is an Apparatus?*, trans. David Kishik and Stefan Pedatella (Stanford: Stanford University Press, 2009), 31.

31 Agamben, *What Is an Apparatus?*, 32.
32 Agamben, *What Is an Apparatus?*, xx.
33 Agamben, *What Is an Apparatus?*, 35.
34 Agamben, *What Is an Apparatus?*, 36.
35 Agamben, *Coming Community*, 105.
36 See Charyl I. Harris, "Whiteness as Property," *Harvard Law Review*, vol. 106, no. 8 (1993): 1707–91.
37 Richard R. Valencia, *The Evolution of Deficit Thinking: Educational Thought and Practice* (Stanford: Stanford University Press, 1997).

Chapter 5

1 See Peter McLaren, *Rage and Hope: Interviews with Peter McLaren on War, Imperialism, and Critical Pedagogy* (New York: Peter Lang, 2006) and Naomi Hodgson, Joris Vlieghe, and Piotr Zamojski, *Manifesto for a Post-Critical Pedagogy* (Santa Barbara: Punctum Books, 2018) for the critical and post-critical interpretations of hope in educational theory.
2 David Halpin, *Hope and Education: The Role of the Utopian Imagination* (New York: Routledge, 2003).
3 Paulo Freire, *Pedagogy of the Heart*, trans. Donald Macedo and Alexandre Oliveira (London: Continuum, 1998), 107.
4 Freire, *Pedagogy of the Heart*, 45.
5 Henry Giroux, "Beyond Dystopian Education in a Neoliberal Society," *Fast Capitalism*, vol. 10, no. 1 (2013): n.p.
6 bell hooks, *Teaching Community: A Pedagogy of Hope* (New York: Routledge, 2003), xiv.
7 hooks, *Teaching Community*, xiv–xv.
8 Paulo Freire, *Pedagogy of Freedom: Ethics, Democracy, and Civic Courage*, trans. Patrick Clarke (Lanham: Rowman & Littlefield, 2001), 72.
9 Freire, *Pedagogy of the Heart*, 69.
10 Freire, *Pedagogy of the Heart*, 69.
11 bell hooks, *Teaching to Transgress* (New York: Routledge, 1994), 207.
12 hooks, *Teaching Community*, 165.
13 Naomi Hodgson, Joris Vlieghe, Piotr Zamojski, *Manifesto for a Post-Critical Pedagogy* (Berkeley: Punctum Books, 2018).
14 Ann Margaret Sharp, *In Community of Inquiry with Ann Margaret Sharp: Childhood, Philosophy and Education*, ed. Maughn Rollins Gregory and Megan Jane Laverty (New York: Routledge, 2017), 56.
15 Sharp, *In Community of Inquiry with Ann Margaret Sharp*, 57.

16 Sharp, *In Community of Inquiry with Ann Margaret Sharp*, 57.
17 Sharp, *In Community of Inquiry with Ann Margaret Sharp*, 55.
18 Sharp, *In Community of Inquiry with Ann Margaret Sharp*, 53.
19 Ann Margaret Sharp, "What Is a 'Community of Inquiry'?" *Journal of Moral Education*, vol. 16, no. 1 (1987): 37.
20 Giorgio Agamben, *The Use of Bodies*, trans. Adam Kotsko (Stanford: Stanford University Press, 2014), 226.
21 Giorgio Agamben, *Means without End: Notes on Politics*, trans. Vincenzo Binetti and Cesare Casarino (Minneapolis: University of Minnesota Press, 2000), 4.
22 Giorgio Agamben, *Karman: A Brief Treatise on Action, Guilt, and Gesture*, trans. Adam Kotsko (Stanford: Stanford University Press, 2018), 69.
23 Agamben, *Means without End*, 114–15.
24 Agamben, *Means without End*, 79.
25 Giorgio Agamben, *The Coming Community*, trans. Michael Hardt (Minneapolis: University of Minnesota Press, 1993), 43.
26 Agamben, *Coming Community*, 43.
27 Agamben, *Coming Community*, 29.
28 Cited in Igor Jasinski, *Giorgio Agamben: Education without Ends* (Rotterdam: Springer, 2018), 59.
29 Agamben, *Means without End*, 4.
30 Agamben, *Means without End*, 8.
31 Agamben, *Means without End*, 114–15.
32 See Paulo Freire, *Pedagogy of the Oppressed*, trans. Myra Bergman Ramos (New York: Continuum, 2001) and Gert Biesta, *The Beautiful Risk of Education* (New York: Routledge, 2014).
33 Agamben, *Karman*, 40.
34 Agamben, *Karman*, 29.
35 Agamben, *Karman*, 34.
36 Agamben, *Karman*, 63.
37 Nicholas Burbules, "The Tragic Sense of Education," *Teachers College Record*, vol. 91, no. 4 (1990): 469–79; Nicholas Burbules, "Teaching and the Tragic Sense of Education," in *Teaching and Its Predicaments*, ed. Nicholas Burbules and David Hansen (Boulder: Westview Press, 1997).
38 Samuel D. Rocha, *Folk Phenomenology: Education, Study, and the Human Person* (Eugene, OR: Pickwick Publishers, 2015).
39 Agamben, *Karman*, 70–1.
40 Giorgio Agamben, *Pulcinella: Or Entertainment for Children*, trans. Kevin Attell (London: Seagull Books, 2019), 43.
41 Louise Amoore, "The Clown at the Gates of the Camp: Sovereignty, Resistance and the Figure of the Fool," *Security Dialogue*, vol. 44, no. 2 (2013): 93.
42 Agamben, *Pulcinella*, 4.

Chapter 6

1. Charles Bingham and Alexander M. Sidorkin (eds.), *No Education without Relation* (New York: Peter Lang, 2004).
2. Giorgio Agamben, *The Use of Bodies*, trans. Adam Kotsko (Stanford: Stanford University Press, 2014), 272.
3. Agamben, *Use of Bodies*, 237.
4. Ann Margaret Sharp, *In Community of Inquiry with Ann Margaret Sharp: Childhood, Philosophy and Education*, ed. Maughn Rollins Gregory and Megan Jane Laverty (New York: Routledge, 2017), 241.
5. Matthew Lipman, "The Contributions of Philosophy to Deliberative Democracy," in *Teaching Philosophy on the Eve of the Twenty-First Century*, eds. David Evans and Ioanna Kucuradi (Ankara: International Federation of Philosophical Societies, 1998), 6.
6. Agamben, *Use of Bodies*, 278.
7. See for instance Eugenio Echeverria and Patricia Hannam, "The Community of Philosophical Inquiry: A Pedagogical Proposal for Advancing Democracy," in *The Routledge International Handbook of Philosophy for Children*, ed. Maughn Rollins Gregory, Joanna Haynes, and Karin Murris (New York: Routledge, 2016).
8. See Darren Chetty, "The Elephant in the Room: Picturebooks, Philosophy for Children and Racism," *Childhood & Philosophy*, vol. 10, no. 19 (2014): 11–31; Amy Reed-Sandoval and Alain Carmen Sykes, "Taking 'Positionality' Seriously in Philosophy for Children," in *The Routledge International Handbook of Philosophy for Children*, ed. Maughn Rollins Gregory, Joanna Haynes, and Karin Murris (New York: Routledge, 2016).
9. Michael Hardt and Antonio Negri, *Empire* (Cambridge, MA: Harvard University Press, 2001), 255.
10. Hardt and Negri, *Empire*, 258.
11. Michael Hardt and Antonio Negri, *Declaration* (London: Argo-Navis, 2012).
12. Agamben, *Use of Bodies*, 275.
13. Giorgio Agamben, *Remnants of Auschwitz: The Witness and the Archive*, trans. Daniel Heller-Roazen (London: Zone Books, 2002), 14.
14. Agamben, *Remnants*, 19.
15. Giorgio Agamben, *The Coming Community*, trans. Michael Hardt (Minneapolis: University of Minnesota Press, 1993), 85.
16. Agamben, *Coming Community*, 85.
17. Agamben, *Coming Community*, 86.
18. Agamben, *Use of Bodies*, 278.
19. Cited in Louis Althusser, *On the Reproduction of Capital: Ideology and Ideological State Apparatuses*, trans. G.M. Goshgarian (London: Verso, 2014), 105.

20 Ernesto Laclau and Chantal Mouffe, *Hegemony and Socialist Strategy: Towards a Radical Democratic Politics* (London: Verso, 1985).
21 Laclau and Mouffe, *Hegemony*, 153–6.
22 Laclau and Mouffe, *Hegemony*, 155, 190.
23 Michael Hardt and Antonio Negri, *Commonwealth* (Cambridge, MA: Harvard University Press, 2009).
24 Giorgio Agamben, *Means without End: Notes on Politics*, trans. Vincenzo Binetti and Cesare Casarino (Minneapolis: University of Minnesota Press, 2000).
25 Giorgio Agamben, *Nudities*, trans. David Kishik and Stefan Pedatella (Stanford: Stanford University Press, 2010), 11.
26 Agamben, *Nudities*, 11.
27 Giorgio Agamben, *Creation and Anarchy: The Work of Art and the Religion of Capitalism*, trans. Adam Kotsko (Stanford: Stanford University Press, 2019), 61.
28 Anarchy is not a widely discussed topic in P4C literature. One exception is David Kennedy, "Anarchism, Schooling, and Democratic Sensibility," *Studies in Philosophy and Education*, no. 36 (2017): 551–68. While gesturing toward anarchy, democracy ultimately subsumes it, thus instrumentalizing it by assuming a specific political telos. Also see Olivier Michaud and Riku Välitalo, "Authority, Democracy and Philosophy: The Nature and Role of Authority in a Community of Philosophical Inquiry," in *The Routledge International Handbook of Philosophy for Children*, ed. Maughn Rollins Gregory, Joanna Haynes, and Karin Murris (London: Routledge, 2017), 27–33. In this book chapter, the authors argue that strong authority and anarchy must be avoided for a middle path: democracy as shared authority.
29 Agamben, *Means without End*, 115.
30 Agamben, *Means without End*, 85.
31 Agamben, *Means without End*, 9.
32 Agamben, *Means without End*, 10.
33 Naomi Hodgson, Joris Vlieghe, and Piotr Zamojski, *Manifesto for a Post-Critical Pedagogy* (Santa Barbara, CA: Punctum Books, 2018).

References

Agamben, Giorgio. *The Coming Community*, trans. Michael Hardt. Minneapolis: University of Minnesota Press, 1993.

Agamben, Giorgio. *Homo Sacer: Sovereign Power and Bare Life*, trans. Daniel Heller-Roazen. Stanford: Stanford University Press, 1998.

Agamben, Giorgio. *Potentialities: Collected Essays in Philosophy*, trans. Daniel Heller-Roazen. Stanford: Stanford University Press, 1999.

Agamben, Giorgio. *The End of the Poem: Studies in Poetics*, trans. Daniel Heller-Roazen. Stanford: Stanford University Press, 1999.

Agamben, Giorgio. *Means without Ends: Notes on Politics*, trans. Vincenzo Binetti and Cesare Casarino. Minneapolis: University of Minnesota Press, 2000.

Agamben, Giorgio. *Remnants of Auschwitz: The Witness and the Archive*, trans. Daniel Heller-Roazen. London: Zone Books, 2002.

Agamben, Giorgio. *State of Exception*, trans. Kevin Attell. Chicago: University of Chicago Press, 2005.

Agamben, Giorgio. *The Time That Remains: A Commentary on the Letter to the Romans*, trans. Patricia Dailey. Stanford: Stanford University Press, 2005.

Agamben, Giorgio. *Language and Death: The Place of Negativity*, trans. Karen Pinkus and Michael Hardt. Minneapolis: University of Minnesota Press, 2006.

Agamben, Giorgio. *Infancy and History: On the Destruction of Experience*, trans. Liz Heron. London: Verso, 2007.

Agamben, Giorgio. *Profanations*, trans. Jeff Fort. London: Zone Books, 2007.

Agamben, Giorgio. *What Is an Apparatus?*, trans. David Kishik and Stefan Pedatella. Stanford: Stanford University Press, 2009.

Agamben, Giorgio. *Nudities*, trans. David Kishik and Stefan Pedatella. Stanford: Stanford University Press, 2010.

Agamben, Giorgio. *The Sacrament of Language: An Archeology of the Oath*, trans. Adam Kotsko. Stanford: Stanford University Press, 2011.

Agamben, Giorgio. *The Highest Poverty: Monastic Rules and Form-of-Life*, trans. Adam Kotsko. Stanford: Stanford University Press, 2013.

Agamben, Giorgio. *The Use of Bodies*, trans. Adam Kotsko. Stanford: Stanford University Press, 2014.

Agamben, Giorgio. *The Fire and the Tale*, trans. Lorenzo Chiesa. Stanford: Stanford University Press, 2017.

Agamben, Giorgio. *Karman: A Brief Treatise on Action, Guilt, and Gesture*, trans. Adam Kotsko. Stanford: Stanford University Press, 2018.

Agamben, Giorgio. *The Adventure*, trans. Lorenzo Chiesa. Cambridge: MIT Press, 2018.
Agamben, Giorgio. *What Is Philosophy?*, trans. Lorenzo Chiesa. Stanford: Stanford University Press, 2018.
Agamben, Giorgio. *Creation and Anarchy: The Work of Art and the Religion of Capitalism*, trans. Adam Kotsko. Stanford: Stanford University Press, 2019.
Agamben, Giorgio. *Pulcinella: Or Entertainment for Children*, trans. Kevin Attell. London: Seagull Books, 2019.
Althusser, Louis. *On the Reproduction of Capital: Ideology and Ideological State Apparatuses*, trans. G. M. Goshgarian. London: Verso, 2014.
Amoore, Louise. "The Clown at the Gates of the Camp: Sovereignty, Resistance and the Figure of the Fool." *Security Dialogue* 44, no. 2 (2013): 93–110.
Biesta, Gert. *Beyond Learning: Democratic Education for a Human Future*. Boulder: Paradigm Publishers, 2006.
Biesta, Gert. "Philosophy, Exposure, and Children." In *Philosophy for Children in Transition: Problems and Prospects*, edited by Nancy Vansieleghem and David Kennedy, 137–51. Malden, MA: Wiley-Blackwell, 2012.
Biesta, Gert. *The Beautiful Risk of Education*. New York: Routledge, 2014.
Biggeri, Mario., and Marina Santi. (2012). "The Missing Dimensions of Children's Well-being and Well-becoming in Education Systems: Capabilities and Philosophy for Children." *Journal of Human Development and Capabilities* 13, no. 3 (2012): 373–95.
Bingham, Charles, and Alexander M. Sidorkin (eds.). *No Education without Relation*. New York: Peter Lang, 2004.
Burbules, Nicholas. 'Teaching and the Tragic Sense of Education." In *Teaching and Its Predicaments*, edited by Nicholas Burbules and David Hansen, 65–77. Boulder: Westview Press, 1997.
Burbules, Nicholas. "The Tragic Sense of Education." *Teachers College Record* 91, no. 4 (1990): 469–79.
Chetty, Darren. "The Elephant in the Room: Picturebooks Philosophy for Children and Racism." *Childhood & Philosophy* 10, no. 19 (2014): 11–31.
Cott, Joanathan. *Conversations with Glenn Gould*. Chicago: University of Chicago Press, 2005.
Darder, Antonia. *Reinventing Paulo Freire: A Pedagogy of Love*. New York: Routledge, 2017.
Dean, Jodi. *Democracy and Other Neoliberal Fantasies: Communicative Capitalism and Left Politics*. Durham: Duke University Press, 2009.
Echeverria, Eugenio, and Patricia Hannam, "The Community of Philosophical Inquiry: A Pedagogical Proposal for Advancing Democracy." In *The Routledge International Handbook of Philosophy for Children*, edited by Maughn Rollins Gregory, Joanna Haynes, and Karin Murris, 3–10. New York: Routledge, 2016.
Freire, Paulo. *Pedagogy of the Heart*, trans. Donald Macedo and Alexandre Oliveira. London: Continuum, 1998.
Freire, Paulo. *Pedagogy of Freedom: Ethics, Democracy, and Civic Courage*, trans. Patrick Clarke. Lanham: Rowan and Littlefield, 2000.

Freire, Paulo. *Pedagogy of the Oppressed*, trans. Myra Bergman Ramos. New York: Continuum, 2001.

Giroux, Henry. "Beyond Dystopian Education in a Neoliberal Society." *Fast Capitalism* 10, no. 1 (2013): n. p.

Gregory, Maughn Rollins (ed.). *Philosophy for Children Practitioner Handbook*. Montclair: IAPC, 2008.

Gregory, Maughn Rollins, Haynes, Joanna, and Karin Murris. "Editorial Introduction: Philosophy for Children: An Educational and Philosophical Movement." In *The Routledge International Handbook of Philosophy for Children*, edited by Maughn Rollins Gregory, Joanna Haynes, and Karin Murris, xxi–xxxi. London: Routledge, 2017.

Halpin, David. *Hope and Education: The Role of the Utopian Imagination*. New York: Routledge, 2003.

Hardt, Michael, and Antonio Negri. *Empire*. Cambridge: Harvard University Press, 2001.

Hardt, Michael, and Antonio Negri. *Commonwealth*. Cambridge: Harvard University Press, 2009.

Hardt, Michael, and Antonio Negri. *Declaration*. London: Argo-Navis, 2012.

Harris, Charyl I. "Whiteness as Property." *Harvard Law Review* 106, no. 8 (1993): 1707–91.

Hodgson, Naomi, Joris Vlieghe, and Piotr Zamojski. *Manifesto for a Post-Critical Pedagogy*. Santa Barbara: Punctum Books, 2018.

hooks, bell. *Teaching to Transgress: Education as the Practice of Freedom*. New York: Routledge, 1994.

hooks, bell. *Teaching Community: A Pedagogy of Hope*. New York: Routledge, 2003.

Illich, Ivan. *Deschooling Society*. London: Marion Boyars, 1970.

Jackson, Thomas. "Philosophical Rules of Engagement." In *Philosophy in Schools: An Introduction for Philosophers and Teachers*, edited by Sara Goering, Nicholas J. Shudak, and Thomas Wartenberg, 99–109. New York: Routledge, 2013.

Jasinski, Igor. *Giorgio Agamben: Education without Ends*. Chalm, Switzerland: Springer, 2018.

Kennedy, David. "The Five Communities." *Analytic Teaching* 15, no. 1 (1994): 3–16.

Kennedy, David. *Philosophical Dialogue with Children: Essays on Theory and Practice*. Lewiston. Edwin Mellen Press, 2010.

Kennedy, David. "Anarchism, Schooling, and Democratic Sensibility." *Studies in Philosophy and Education* 36, no. 5 (2017): 551–68.

Kennedy, Nadia, and David Kennedy. "Community of Philosophical Inquiry as a Discursive Structure and Its Role in School Curriculum Design." *Journal of Philosophy of Education* 45, no. 2 (2011): 265–83.

Kohan, Walter Omar. "Childhood, Education and Philosophy: Notes on Deterritorialisation." In *Philosophy for Children in Transition: Problems and Prospects*, edited by Nancy Vansieleghem and David Kennedy, 170–89. Walden, MA: Wiley-Blackwell, 2012.

Kohan, Walter Omar. *Childhood, Education and Philosophy: New Ideas for an Old Relationship*. New York: Routledge, 2014.
Laclau, Ernesto, and Chantal Mouffe. *Hegemony and Socialist Strategy: Towards a Radical Democratic Politics*. London: Verso, 1985.
Lewis, Tyson E. "The School as an Exceptional Space: Rethinking Education from the Perspective of the Biopedagogical." *Educational Theory* 56, no. 2 (2006): 159–76.
Lewis, Tyson E. *On Study: Giorgio Agamben and Educational Potentiality*. New York: Routledge, 2013.
Lewis, Tyson. E. *Inoperative Learning: A Radical Rewriting of Educational Potentialities*. New York: Routledge, 2017.
Lindop, Clive. "Harry 17: Judgement, Perspective and Philosophy." *Thinking: The Journal of Philosophy for Children* 8, no. 3 (1989): 39–40.
Lipman, Matthew. *Philosophy Goes to School*. Philadelphia: Temple University Press, 1988.
Lipman, Matthew. "Pixie and the Relationship between Cognitive Modelling and Cognitive Practice." In *Studies in Philosophy for Children: Pixie*, edited by Ronald F. Reed and Ann M. Sharp, 28–36. Madrid: Ediciones de la Torre, 1996.
Lipman, Matthew. "The Contributions of Philosophy to Deliberative Democracy." In *Teaching Philosophy on the Eve of the Twenty-First Century*, edited by David Evans and Ioanna Kucuradi, 6–29. Ankara: International Federation of Philosophical Societies, 1998.
Lipman, Matthew. *Thinking in Education*. New York: Cambridge University Press, 2003.
Lipman, Matthew, and Ann Margaret Sharp. "Some Educational Presuppositions for Philosophy for Children." *Oxford Review of Education* 4, no. 11 (1978): 85–90.
Lipman, Matthew, Ann Margaret Sharp, and Frederick S. Oscanyan. *Philosophy in the Classroom*. Philadelphia, PA: Temple University Press, 1980.
Masschelein, Jan, and Maarten Simons. "School as Architecture for Newcomers and Strangers: The Perfect School as Public School?" *Teachers College Record* 112, no. 10 (2010): 535–55.
Masschelein, Jan, and Maarten Simons. *In Defense of the School: A Public Issue*, trans. Jack McMartin. Leuven: Education, Culture & Society, 2013.
Matthews, Gareth B. *Philosophy and the Young Child*. Cambridge: Harvard University Press, 1980.
McLaren, Peter. *Che Guevara, Paulo Freire, and the Pedagogy of Revolution*. London: Rowan & Littlefield Publishers, 2000.
McLaren, Peter. *Rage and Hope: Interviews with Peter McLaren on War, Imperialism, and Critical Pedagogy*. New York: Peter Lang, 2006.
Michaud, Olivier, and Riku Välitalo. "Authority, Democracy and Philosophy: The Nature and Role of Authority in a Community of Philosophical Inquiry." In *The Routledge International Handbook of Philosophy for Children*, edited by Maughn Rollins Gregory, Joanna Haynes, and Karin Murris, 27–33. London: Routledge, 2017.
Murris, Karin S. "Philosophy with Children, the Stingray and the Educative Value of Disequilibrium." *Journal of Philosophy of Education* 42, no. 3–4 (2008): 667–85.

Reed-Sandoval, Amy, and Alain Carmen Sykes. "'Who Talks? Who Listens? Taking 'Positionality' Seriously in Philosophy for Children." In *The Routledge International Handbook of Philosophy for Children*, edited by Maughn Rollins Gregory, Joanna Haynes, and Karin Murris, 219–26. New York: Routledge, 2016.

Reznitskaya, Alina, and Ian A. G. Wilkinson. *The Most Reasonable Answer: Helping Students Build Better Arguments Together*. Cambridge: Harvard University Press, 2017.

Reznitskaya, Alina, and Richard C. Anderson. "Analyzing Argumentation in Rich, Natural Contexts." *Informal Logic* 26, no. 2 (2006): 175–98.

Reznitskaya, Alina, Monica Glina, Brian Carolan, Olivier Michaud, Jon Rogers, and Lavina Sequeira. "Examining Transfer Effects from Dialogic Discussions to New Tasks and Contexts." *Contemporary Educational Psychology* 37, no. 4 (2012): 288–306.

Rocha, Samuel D. *Folk Phenomenology: Education, Study, and the Human Person*. Eugene, OR: Pickwick Publishers, 2015.

Sharp, Ann Margaret. "What Is a 'Community of Inquiry'?" *Journal of Moral Education* 16, no. 1 (1987): 37–45.

Sharp, Ann Margaret. "Self-transformation in the Community of Inquiry." In *In Community of Inquiry with Ann Margaret Sharp: Childhood, Philosophy and Education*, edited by Maughn Rollins Gregory and Megan Jane Laverty, 49–59. New York: Routledge, 2017.

Sharp, Ann Margaret. "Silence and Speech in *Pixie*." In *In Community of Inquiry with Ann Margaret Sharp: Childhood, Philosophy and Education*, edited by Maughn Rollins Gregory and Megan Jane Laverty, 174–85. New York: Routledge, 2017.

Sharp, Ann Margaret, and Megan Jane Laverty. "Looking at Others' Faces." In *In Community of Inquiry with Ann Margaret Sharp: Childhood, Philosophy and Education*, edited by Maughn Rollins Gregory and Megan Jane Laverty, 120–30. New York: Routledge, 2017.

Sharp, Ann Margaret, and Megan Jane Laverty. "The Community of Inquiry: Education for Democracy." In *In Community of Inquiry with Ann Margaret Sharp: Childhood, Philosophy and Education*, edited by Maughn Rollins Gregory and Megan Jane Laverty, 241–50. New York: Routledge, 2017.

Siepmann, Jeremy. "Glenn Gould and the Interpreter's Prerogative." *The Musical Times* 131, no. 1763 (1990): 25–7.

Simons, Maarten. "Learning as Investment: Notes on Governmentality and Biopolitics." *Educational Philosophy and Theory* 38, no. 4 (2006): 523–40.

Simons, Maarten, and Jan Masschelein. "The Learning Society and Governmentality: An Introduction." *Educational Philosophy and Theory* 38, no. 4 (2006): 417–30.

Storme, Thomas, and Joris Vlieghe. "The Experience of Childhood and the Learning Society." In *Philosophy for Children in Transition: Problems and Prospects*, edited by Nancy Vansieleghem and David Kennedy, 13–29. Malden, MA: Wiley-Blackwell, 2012.

Valencia, Richard R. *The Evolution of Deficit Thinking: Educational Thought and Practice*. Stanford: Stanford University Press, 1997.

Vansieleghem, Nancy. "Philosophy for Children as the Wind of Thinking." *Journal of Philosophy of Education* 39, no. 1 (2005): 19–35.

Vansieleghem, Nancy. "Philosophy with Children as an Exercise in Parrhesia: An Account of a Philosophical Experiment with Children in Cambodia." In *Philosophy for Children in Transition: Problems and Prospects*, edited by Nancy Vansieleghem and David Kennedy, 152–69. Malden, MA: Wiley-Blackwell, 2012.

Vansieleghem, Nancy, and David Kennedy. "Introduction: What Is Philosophy for Children, What Is Philosophy with Children—After Matthew Lipman?" In *Philosophy for Children in Transition: Problems and Prospects*, edited by Nancy Vansieleghem and David Kennedy, 1–12. Malden, MA: Wiley-Blackwell, 2012.

Vlieghe, Joris, and Piotr Zamojski. *Towards an Ontology of Teaching: Thing-Centred Pedagogy, Affirmation, and Love for the World*. Rotterdam: Springer, 2019.

Index

adventure 15–16, 61–76, 112, 114–5
anarchy 17–18, 117–36, 148 n.28
Aristotle 7, 85–6, 91–2, 103, 106, 111

Biesta, Gert J. J. 1, 3, 109
blasphemy 28, 30–1, 32, 40, 42, 63, 69
blessing 26, 28, 84, 95

clown, as teacher 22, 40, 113–14
command 14, 15, 33, 35, 36, 122–3, 133–5
communicative capitalism 29, 122–3, 13–4
contact 18–19, 117–19, 123, 126, 130–3, 134, 135, 136
contact/relationality 23, 117–18, 122, 123, 128
contemplation 8, 36, 37, 54–6, 62, 71, 103, 105, 111, 114, 125–6, 132
curse 27–9

experimentum linguae 5, 74
exposure 3, 54, 56, 66, 76, 87, 89, 101

form-of-life 17, 49–50, 53, 54, 102, 107
Franciscan Order 48, 107
Freire, Paulo 78, 80–1, 98–9, 109
friendship 77, 91–6, 106

Gould, Glenn 88–9, 91

happiness 16–17, 97–115
Hardt, Michael 120–1, 128
hooks, bell 78, 98, 99
hope 16–17, 18, 97–100, 104, 107–9

identity 16, 33, 56, 66, 79, 83, 85, 86–7, 90, 92, 94–6, 104, 107, 125
Illich, Ivan 21–2, 31, 48
impotentiality 7–8, 81, 85–6, 89–90, 102, 111–12

infancy 6, 8, 9, 35–6, 42–3, 64, 74, 76, 135
infrastructure 17, 18, 119, 123, 126, 128–9, 130–1, 133, 135–6
inoperative 5, 9, 12, 13, 30, 50, 59, 63, 69, 71, 73, 104, 112, 129, 131, 135
instrumentalization 11, 13, 17, 47, 71, 119, 123

Kennedy, David 46, 51, 53–4, 78, 148 n.28

Laclau, Ernesto 127–8
law 48–60, 68, 70–1, 113–14, 124, 135
learning 1, 3, 13, 57–60, 68, 71, 104, 120–2, 127, 128
learning society 1, 11, 104, 106, 120–3
Lenin, V. I. 127
Lipman, Matthew 2, 4, 9–14, 32–3, 41, 46–7, 51–2, 61–3, 68, 69, 73, 75–6, 77–8, 118
love 16, 76, 77–85, 90–6

manners 16, 87–8, 93–4, 105, 112
Marxism 128–9, 130, 131
Masschelein, Jan 21–2, 31, 48
May '68, 123–4, 127
McLaren, Peter 78
messianic 4, 5, 9, 13, 71, 102
Mouffe, Chantal 127–8

Negri, Antonio 120–1, 128

oath 14, 22–3, 26–35, 40, 63, 80, 83–4, 121, 135

Plato 78, 80, 81, 103
Post-Marxism 128, 129, 130, 131
potentiality 4–5, 6–7, 8, 9, 55–6, 81–3, 85–6, 91, 96, 100–2, 104–5, 111, 130
profanation 22, 48, 70
Pulcinella 112–13

reasonableness 2–3, 12, 34, 36, 37, 38–39, 40, 53, 54, 56, 67–8, 69, 78, 101
rule 14–15, 45–60, 65, 107

Sharp, Ann M. 2, 12–13, 51, 62, 63, 68, 100–2, 118, 134
Simons, Maarten 21–22, 31, 48
Socrates 111
studious play 62, 67–73

Tiananmen Square 18, 119–20, 123, 124–6, 130–2

Voice 14, 22, 23–31, 32–8, 52, 57, 74, 93

whatever 16, 55, 78–9, 84–93, 95–6

www.ingramcontent.com/pod-product-compliance
Lightning Source LLC
Chambersburg PA
CBHW061841300426
44115CB00013B/2463